I0484916

Owen Sound Ontario Book 2 in Colour Photos, Saving Our History One Photo at a Time

Photography
by Barbara Raué
2014

Series Name:
Cruising Ontario

Book 93: Owen Sound

Cover photo: Knox United Church

Series Name: Cruising Ontario
Saving Our History One Photo at a Time
in colour photos

Other Books by Barbara Raue

Coins of Gold

Arrows, Indians and Love

The Life and Times of Barbara
Volume 1: Inventions That Have Enhanced My Life
Volume 2: Entertainment That I Have Enjoyed
Volume 3: East Coast Trips
Volume 4: Olympics Have Always Intrigued Me
Volume 5: Wonders of the World
Volume 6: Caribbean Cruises We Have Enjoyed
Volume 7: Animals
Volume 8: Storms and Other Major Disasters in My Lifetime
Volume 9: Wars, Terrorist Attacks and Major Disasters

The Cromwell Family Book

Laura Secord Discovered

Visit Barbara's website to view all of her books
http://barbararaue.ca

Owen Sound is located on the southern shores of Georgian Bay in a valley below the sheer rock cliffs of the Niagara Escarpment. The city is located at the mouths of the Pottawatomi and Sydenham Rivers. It has tree-lined streets, many parks, and tree-covered hillsides and ravines.

In 1814-1818, the first Admiralty Survey of Lake Ontario and the coastal waters of Georgian Bay was undertaken by Captain William Fitzwilliam Owen, Royal Naval Officer, surveyor, land-owner, politician, author and justice of the peace. He named the bay and the future site of Owen Sound after his family. His successor, Admiral Henry Wolsey Bayfield, completed the first survey of lakes Erie, Huron, and Superior in 1817-1825. The work of these officers rendered great service to Canada by increasing the safety of navigation.

The city was first known as Sydenham when it was settled in 1840 by Charles Rankin. Prior to his arrival, the area was inhabited by the Ojibway people. In 1851 the name was changed to Owen Sound. For much of its history, it was a major port city known as the "Chicago of the North."

Owen Sound Bay is a valley in the Niagara Escarpment formed by rivers that cut through the escarpment limestone. The valley begins where the Sydenham River cuts down through the escarpment at Inglis Falls and extends out through the bay beyond Bayview Point for a total distance of 16 kilometres.

As the Niagara Escarpment winds its way across southern Ontario, it is interrupted by many deep valleys carved out by the erosive forces of water and ice. Like Colpoy's Bay to the north, Owen Sound Bay is a drowned valley partially hidden under Georgian Bay. Other escarpment valleys like the Dundas Valley are buried under glacial sediments, while the Beaver and Bighead Valleys are occupied by rivers.

Today the Niagara Escarpment continues to slowly erode back from its present position.

The Photomosaic Project – celebrating 150 years of Owen Sound

This huge mural was unveiled on December 31, 2007. It depicts the Canadian one dollar bill; the currency features two boats which were built at Russell Brothers on the east side of the harbour. The Ancaster is the smaller of the two boats; it was built in 1951 and was used on the Ottawa River where it sank in 1979. It was raised in 1982 and restored; it was returned to Owen Sound in 1991 and is on display at the Owen Sound Marine & Rail Museum.

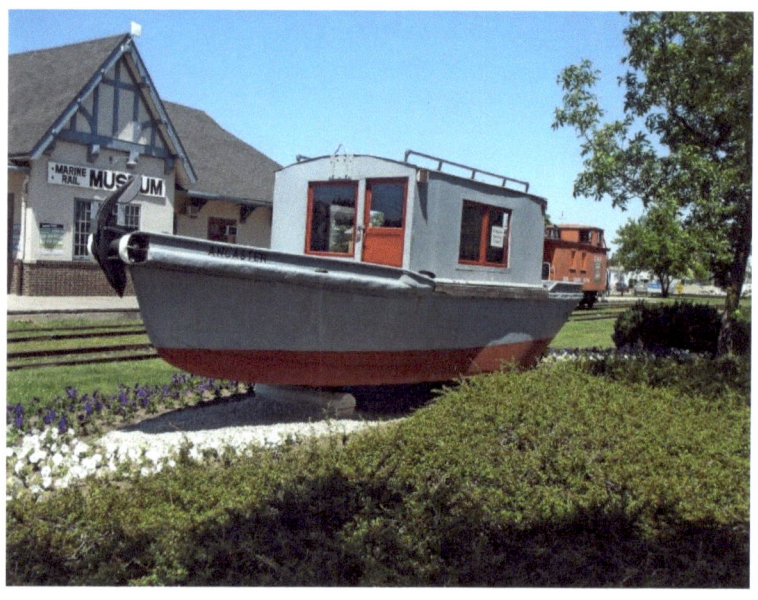

The larger boat, Missinaibi, was built in 1952 and served as a logging boat on the Ottawa River. It is on display at the Museum of Civilization in Hull.

The photomosaic was created by Will McReynolds using 363 photos of Owen Sounders and their families.

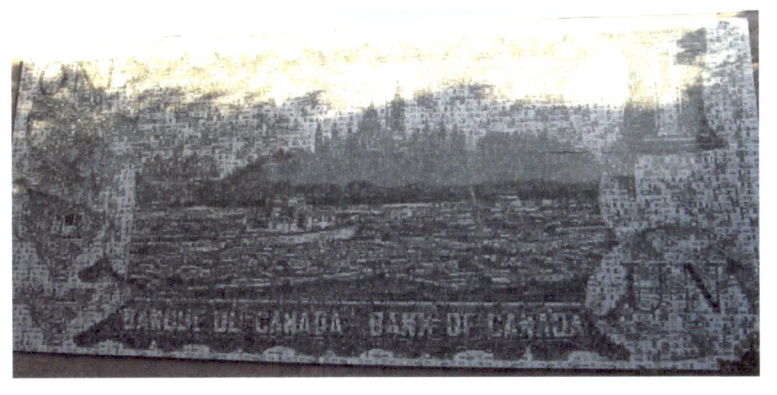

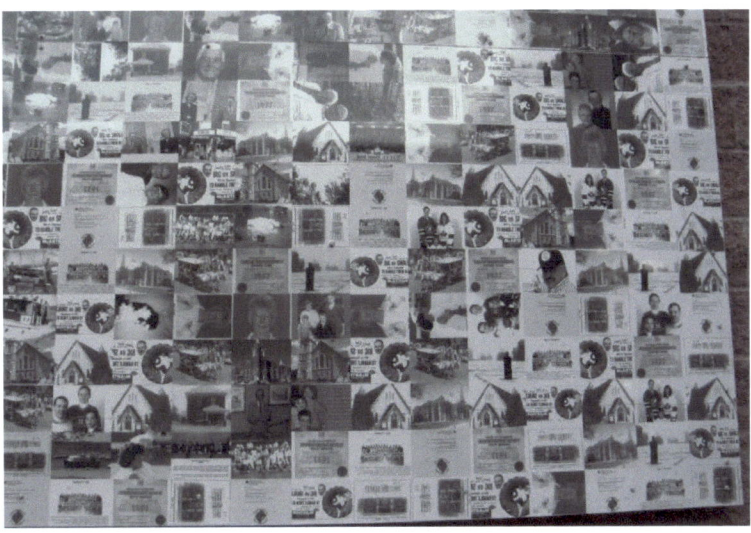

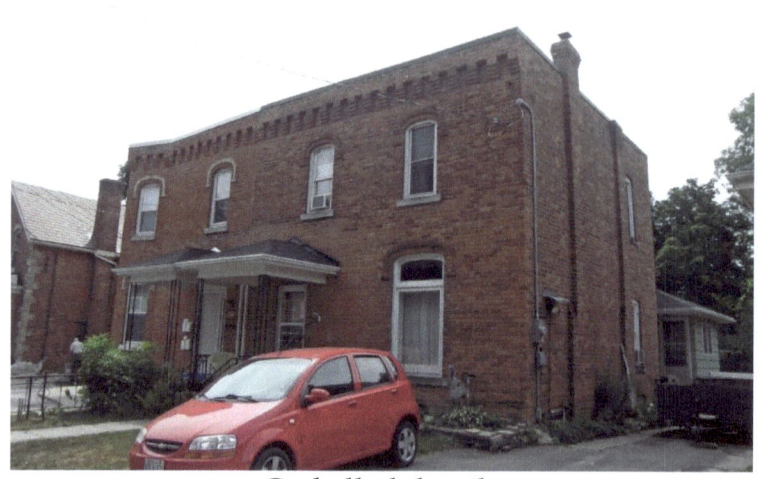

Corbelled dentils

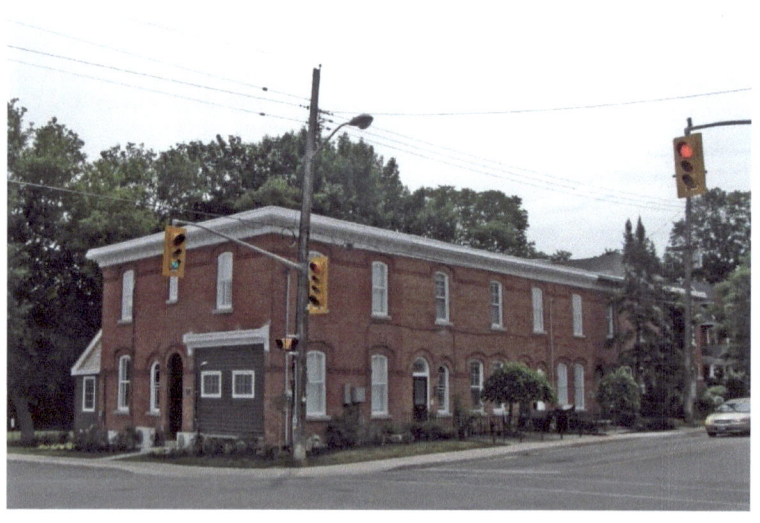

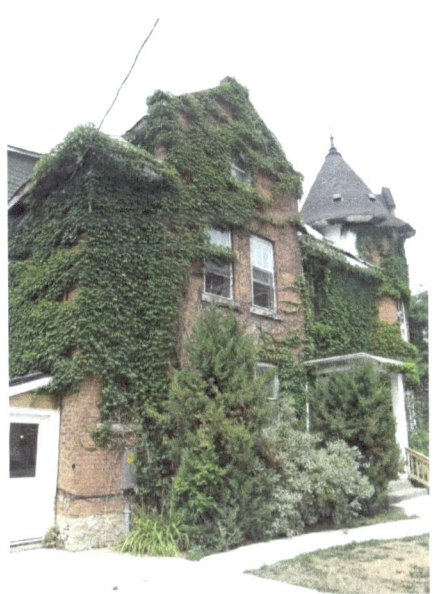

Turret – Queen Anne style

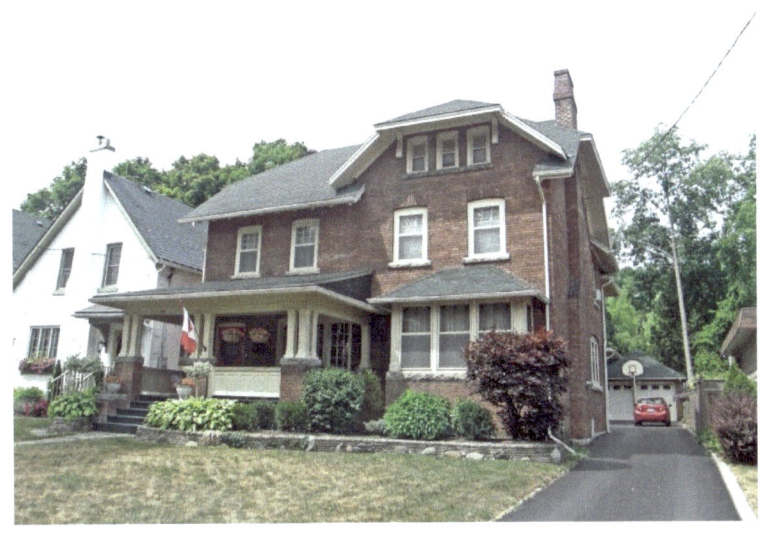

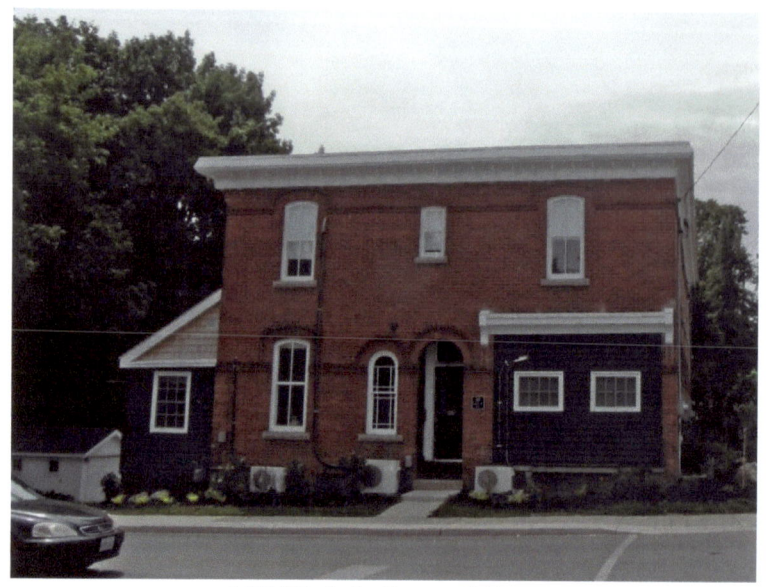

197 Eighth Street West

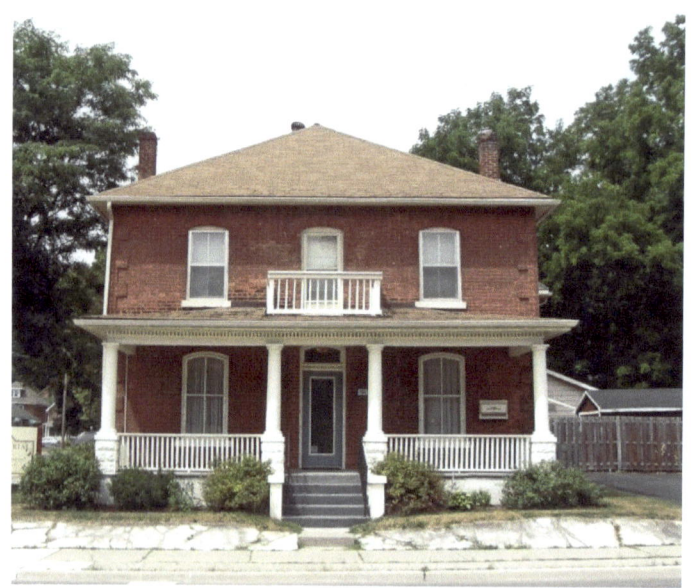

#804 – Italianate, hipped roof, balcony on second floor

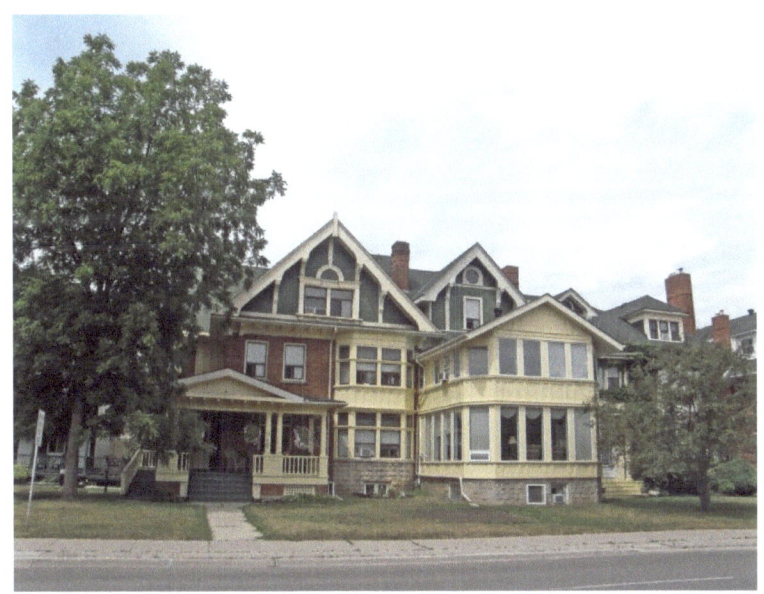

Tudor Revival

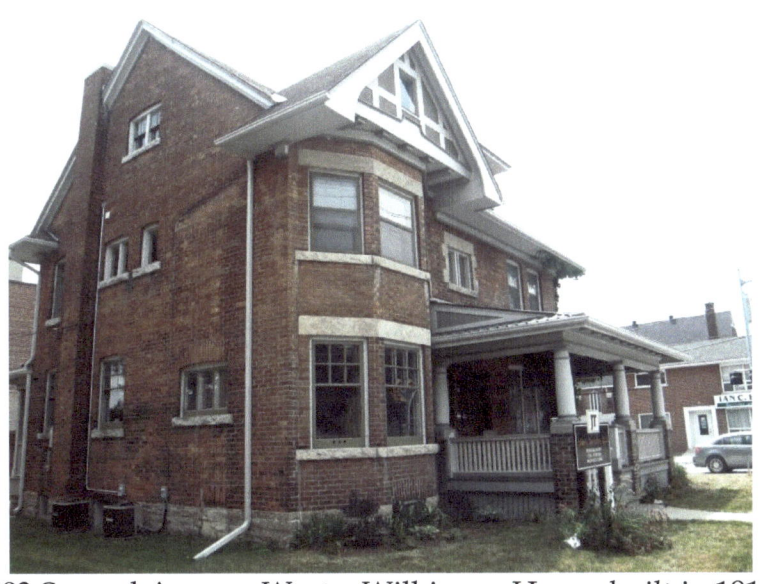

903 Second Avenue West – Wilkinson House built in 1912
Vernacular style

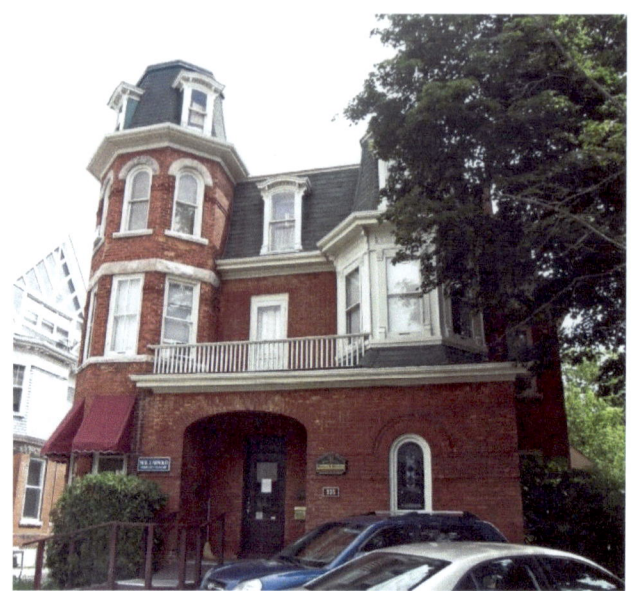

#935 2nd Avenue West – built in 1912, Second Empire style
3-storey turret, mansard roof

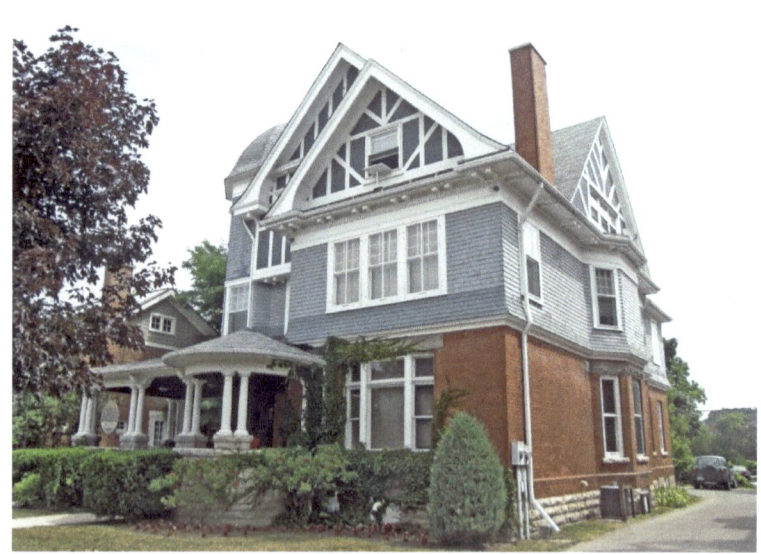

Tudor style

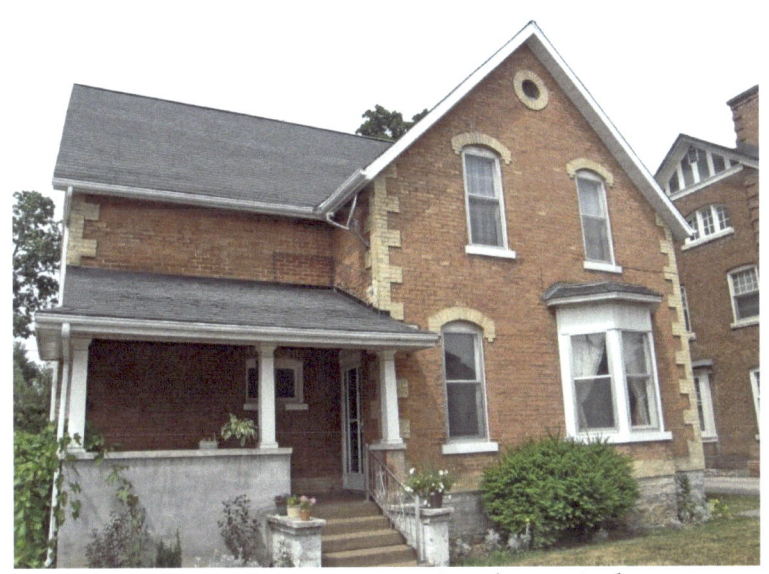

Gothic style, corner quoins, bay window

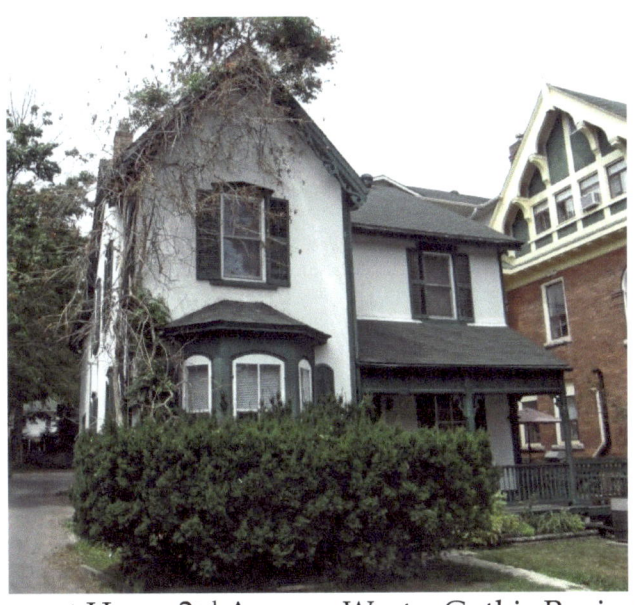

Retirement Home 2nd Avenue West – Gothic Revival, bay window

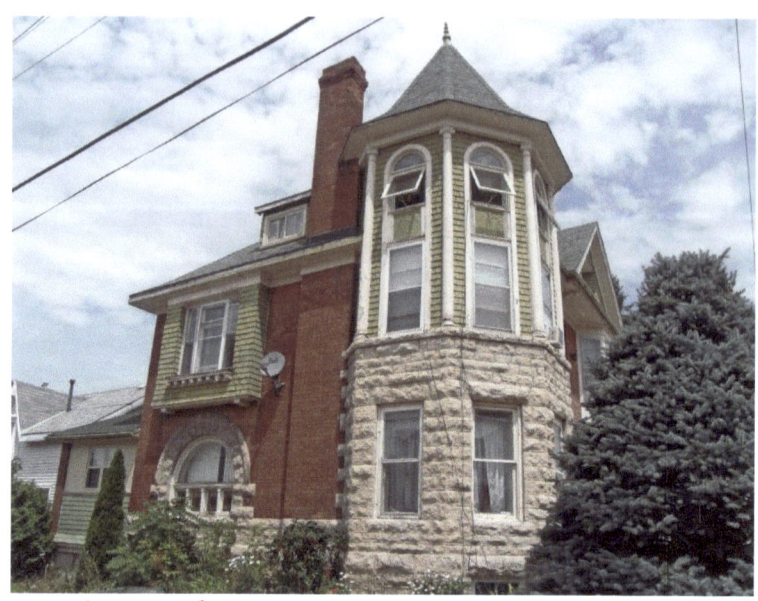

Queen Anne style – turret, Romanesque style window arch

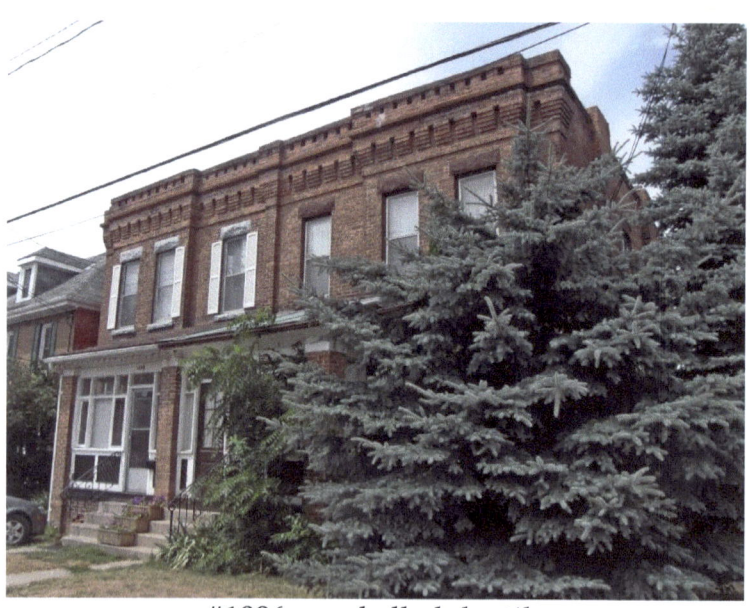

#1096 – corbelled dentils

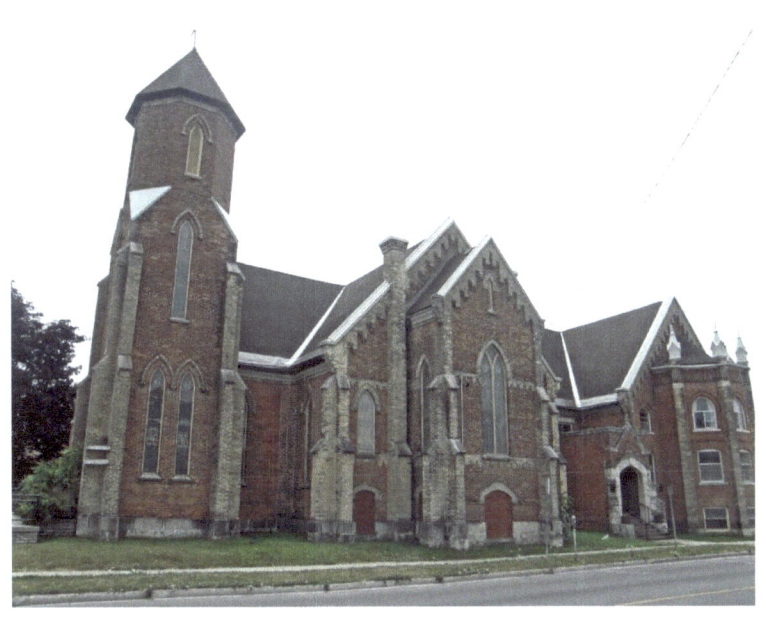

Knox United Church – beautiful rose window

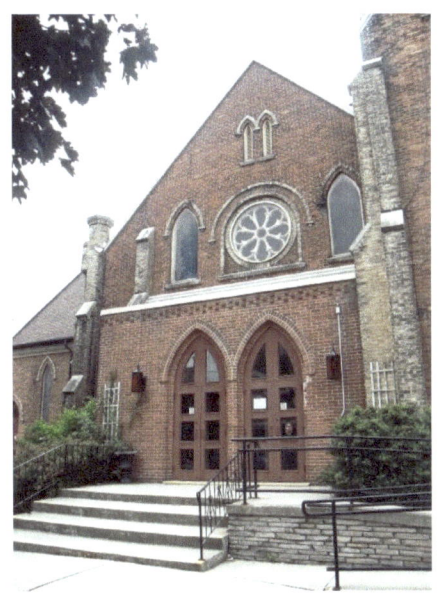

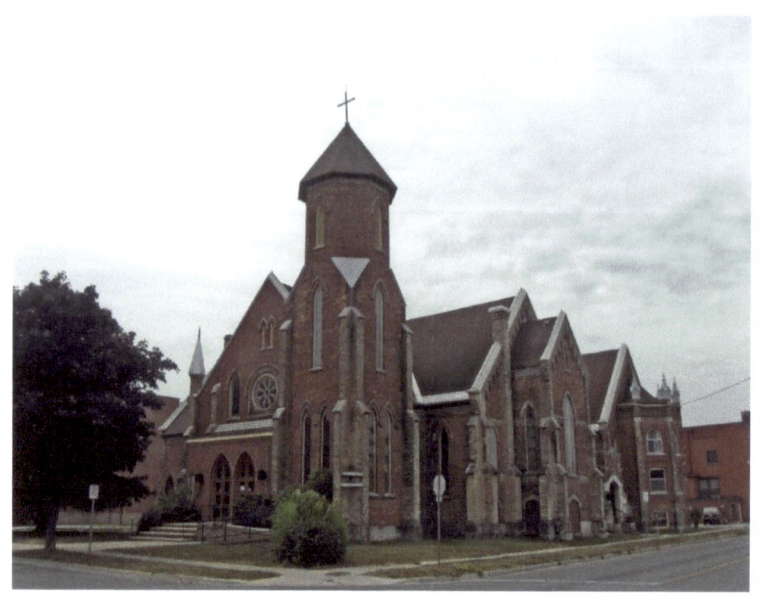

Knox United Church
9th Street East and 4th Avenue

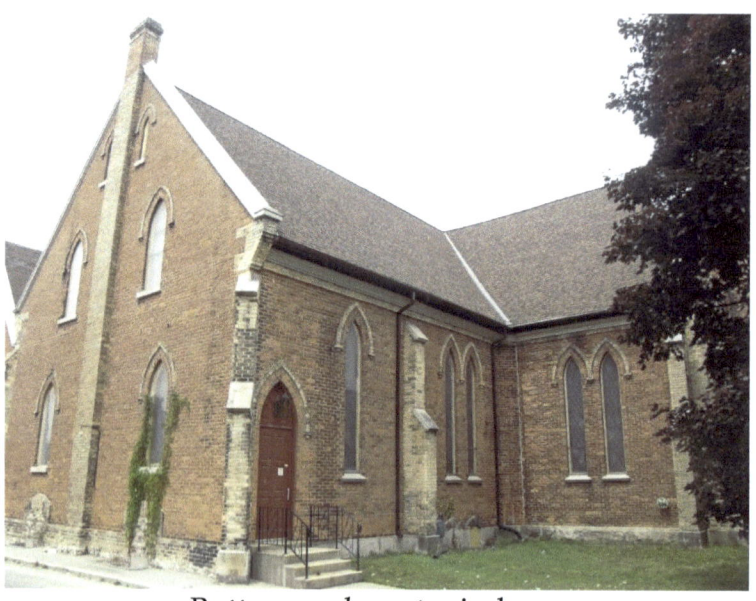

Buttresses, lancet windows

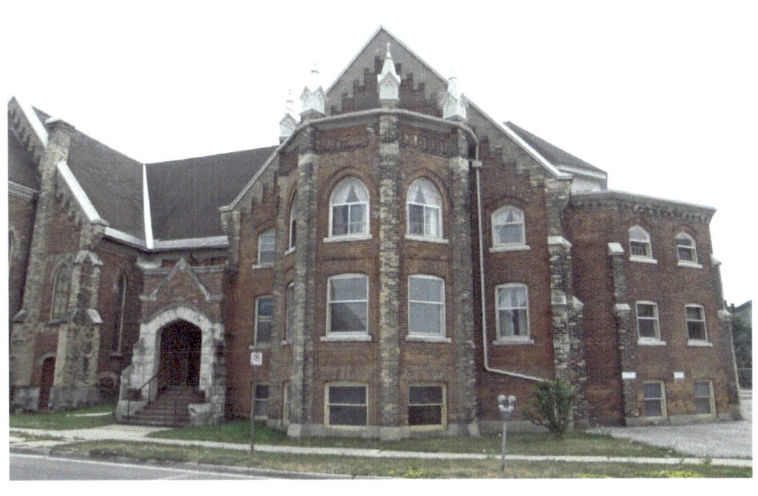

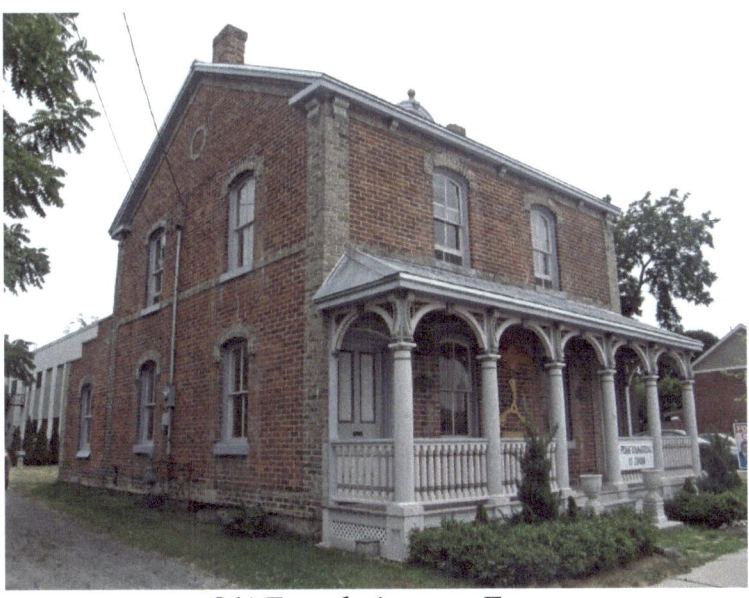

961 Fourth Avenue East

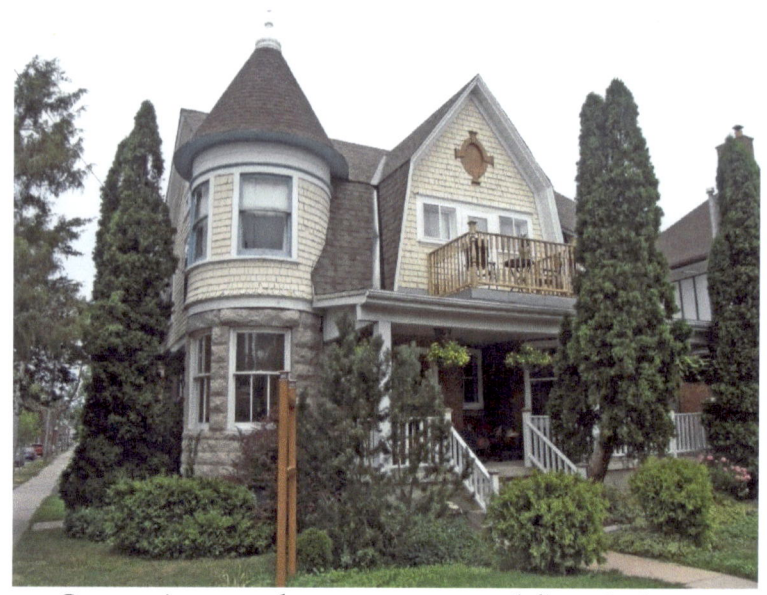

Queen Anne style – turret, second floor balcony

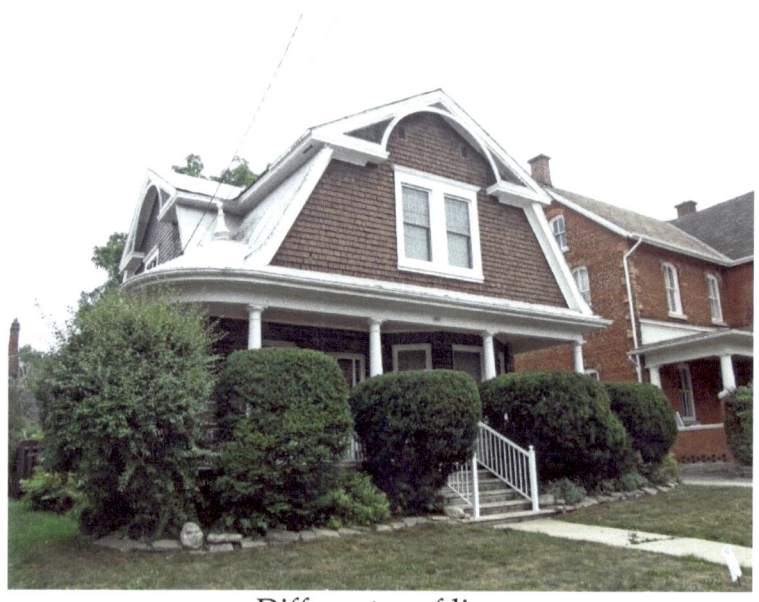

Different roof line

9th Street East and 4th Avenue

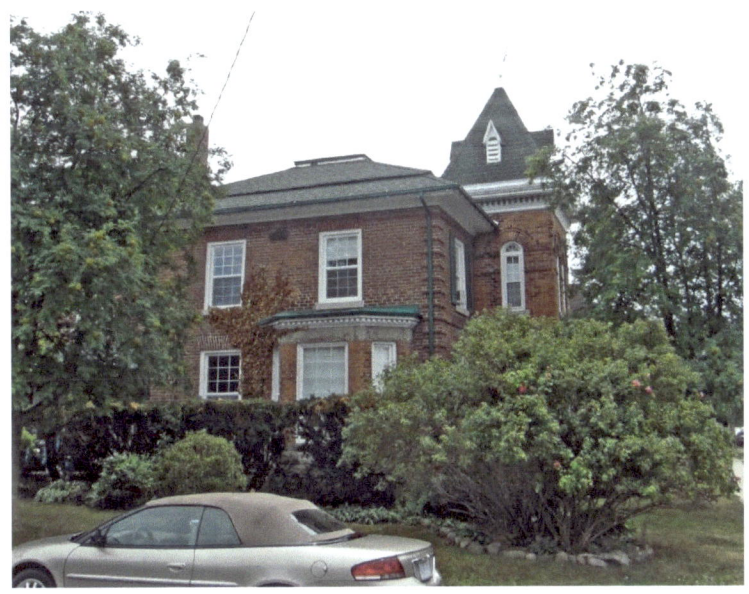

Italianate hipped roof, two storey tower,
corner quoins, bay window

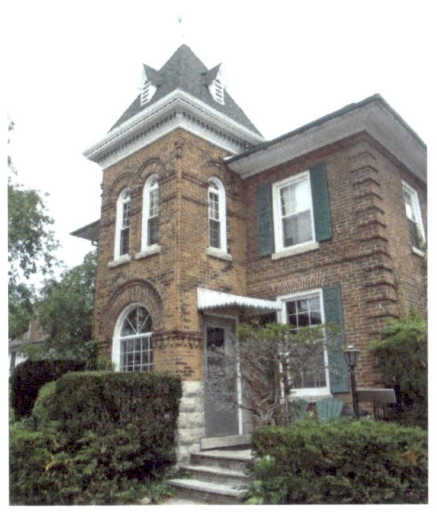

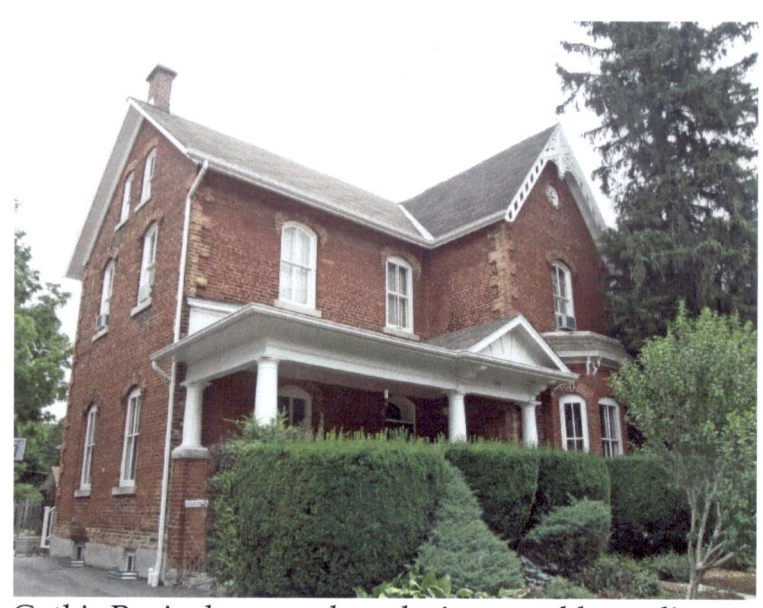

Gothic Revival – verge board trim on gable, pediment, bay window

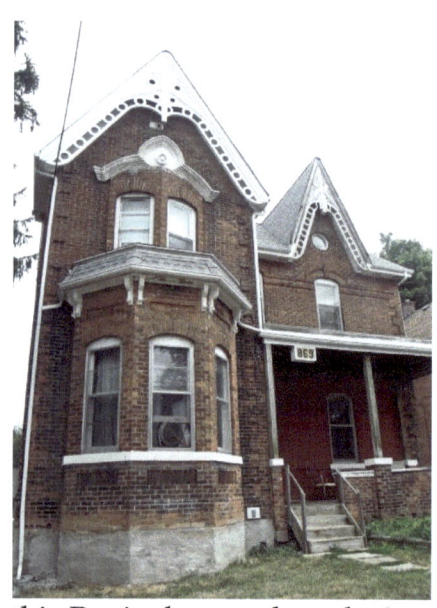

#869 - Gothic Revival, verge board trim on gables, cornice brackets

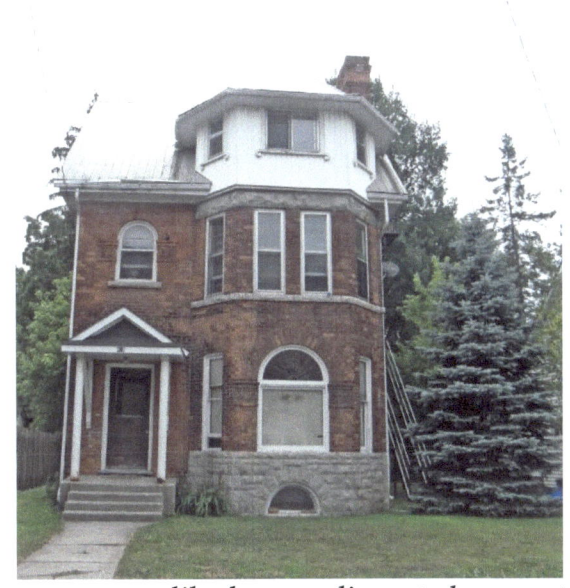

2½ storey tower-like bay, pediment above entrance
Vernacular style

5th Avenue East and 8th Street East

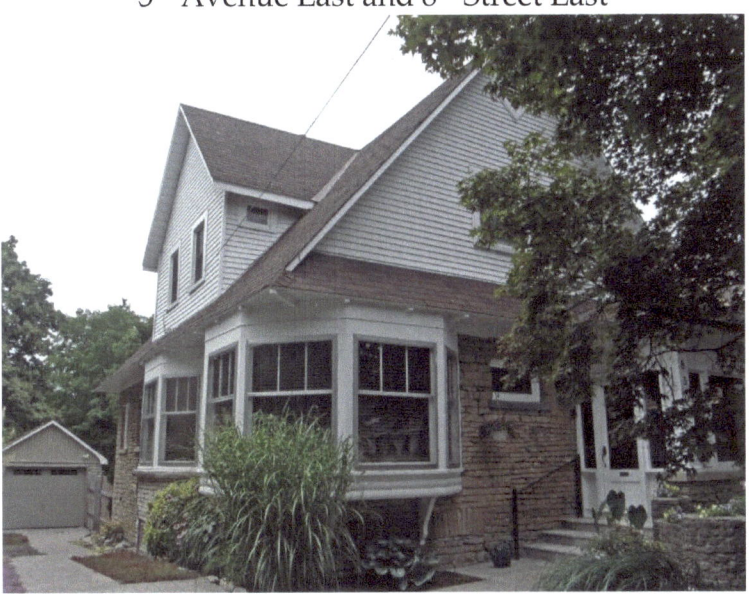

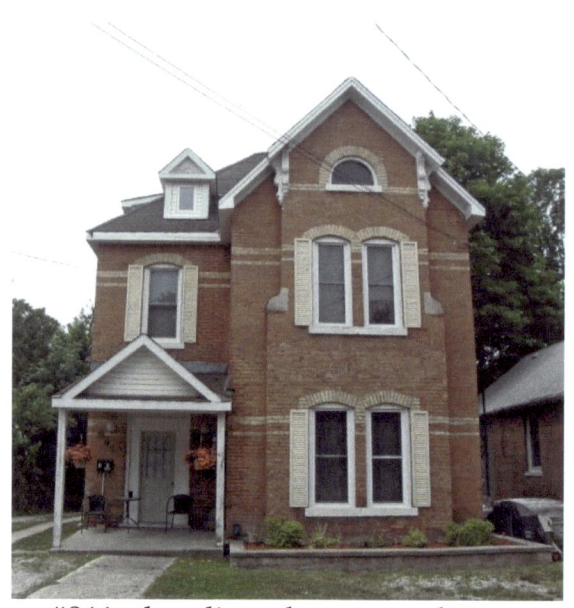

#844 – banding, dormer, pediment

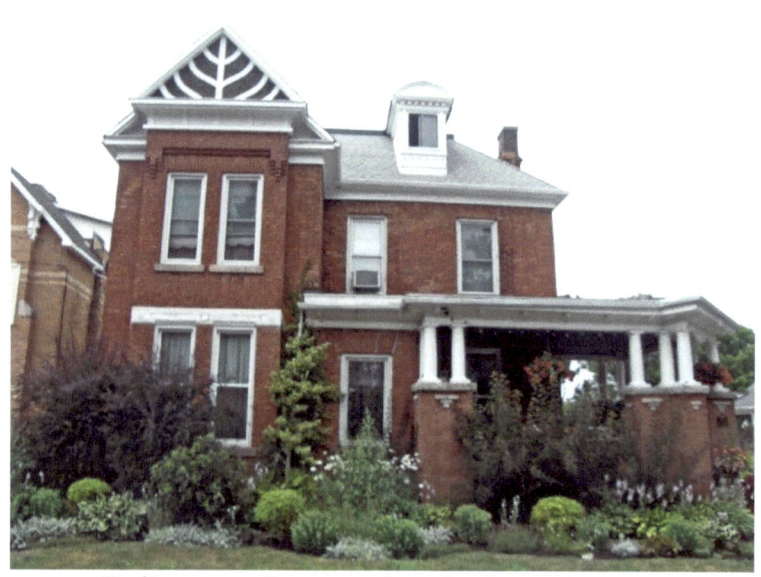

Italianate – 2 storey frontispiece, dormer

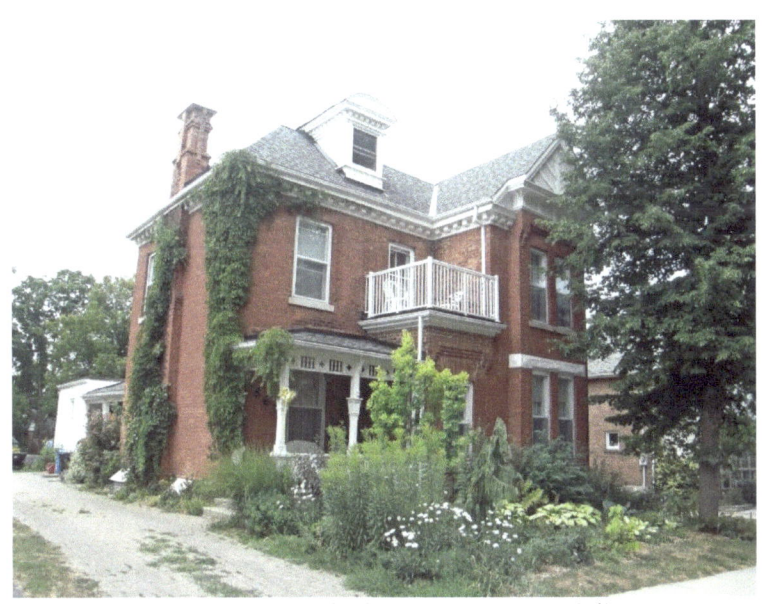

#862 – dormer, balcony on second floor

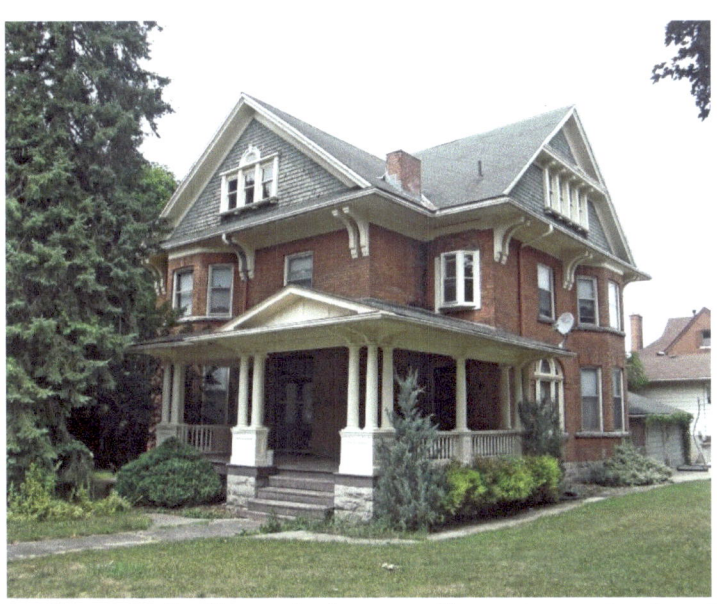

Edwardian – Palladian window, pediment, cornice brackets,
two-storey bay windows

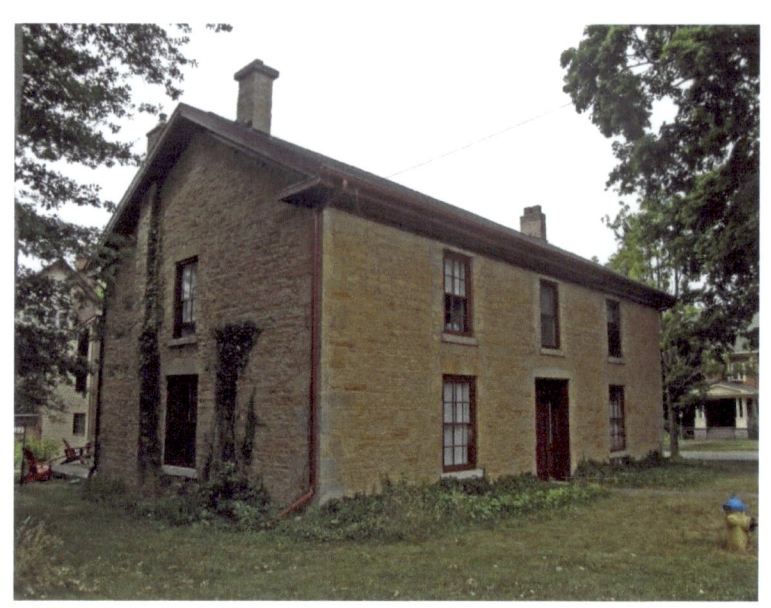

9th Street East 5th Avenue East

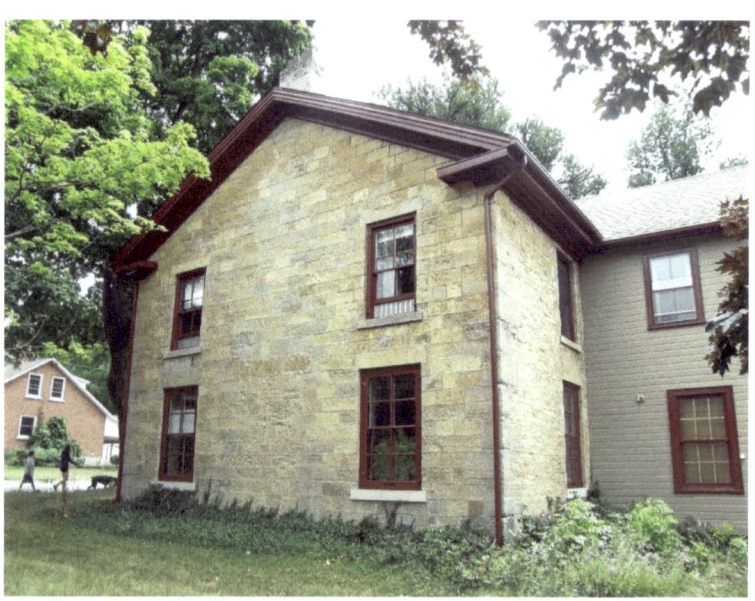

Cornice return on gable

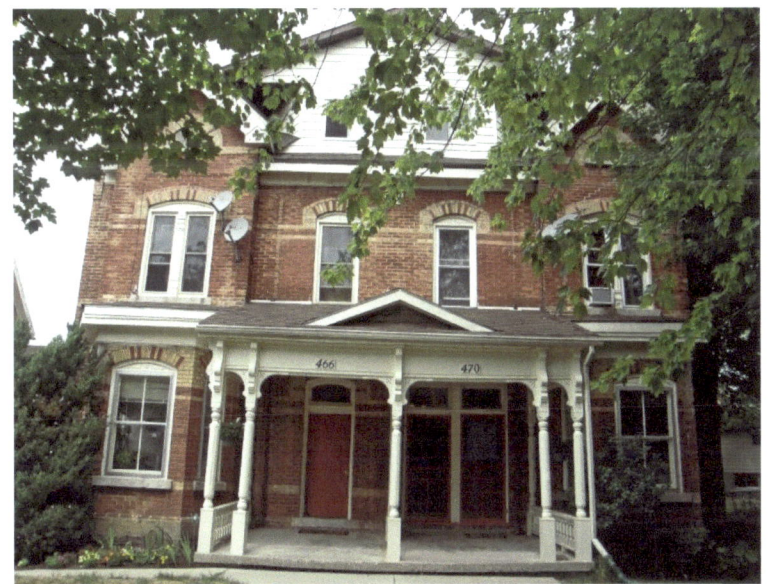

#466 and #470 – dichromatic brickwork, banding, pediment

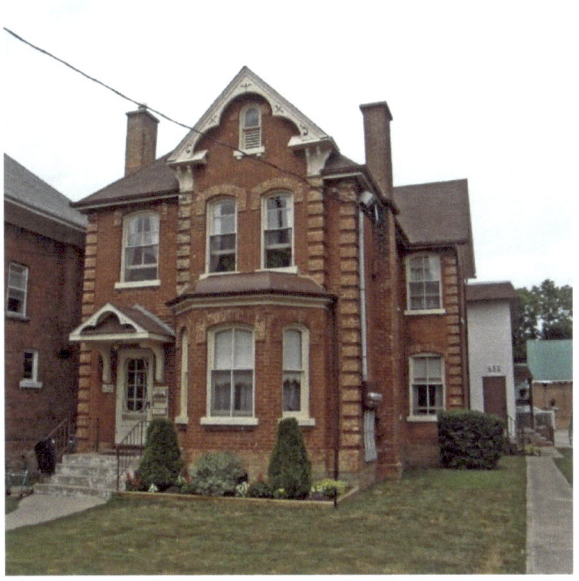

#452 – Gothic style, verge board trim, cornice brackets, corner quoins, bay window

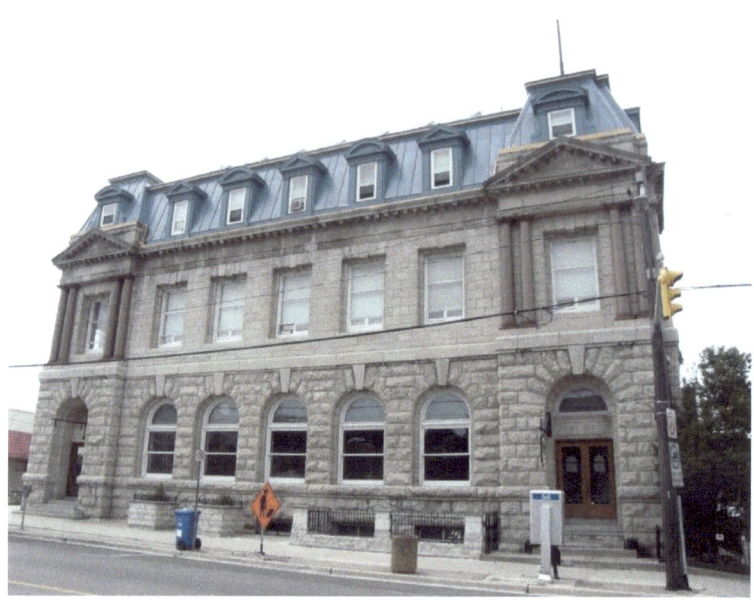

Old Post Office – 1907 – Beaux Arts style featuring harmony
and balance; positioning of windows, Ionic columns,
pediments project vertical and horizontal symmetry; shapes
and materials echo across all three floors in pleasing
proportions; varied texture of stone graduates from rough and
solid rock face limestone to slightly inset and smoother stone
above, providing a lighter feel the higher the building climbs;
window sills are continuous cut stone, walls are lined with
brick; a brick vault was constructed on each of the first and
second floors; mansard roof with dormers; voussoirs and
keystones over windows and doors on first floor,

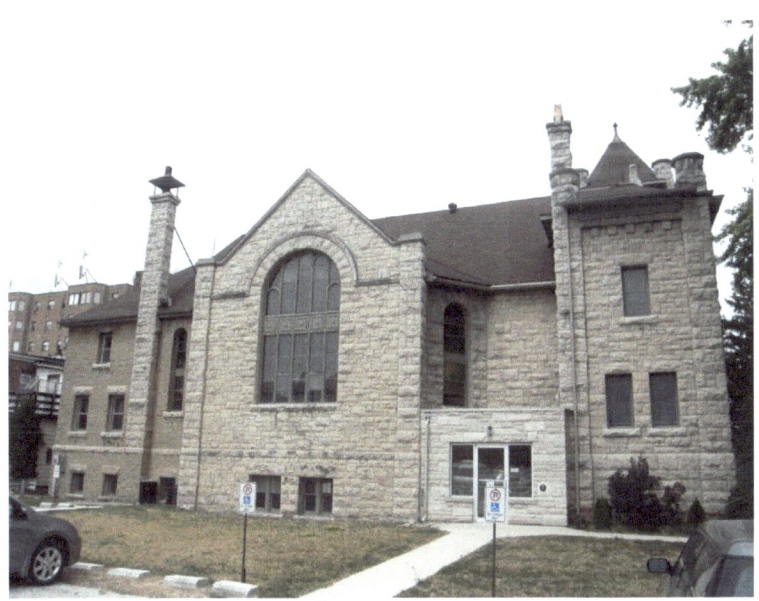

limestone

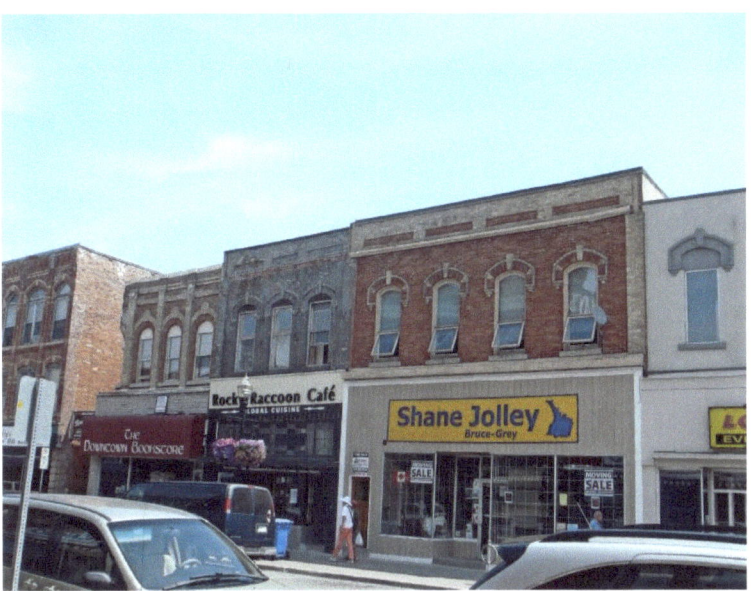

Voussoirs, keystones, dichromatic brickwork

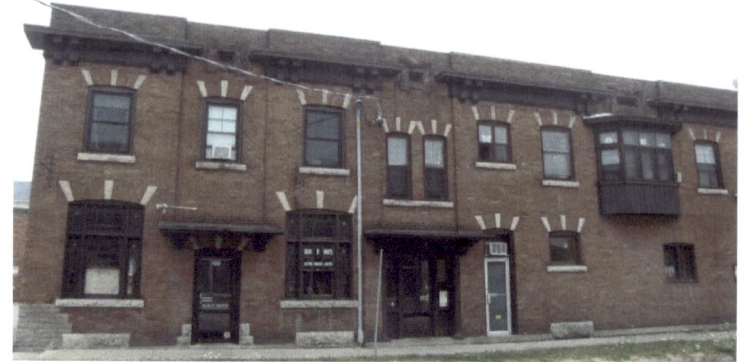

Dichromatic brickwork

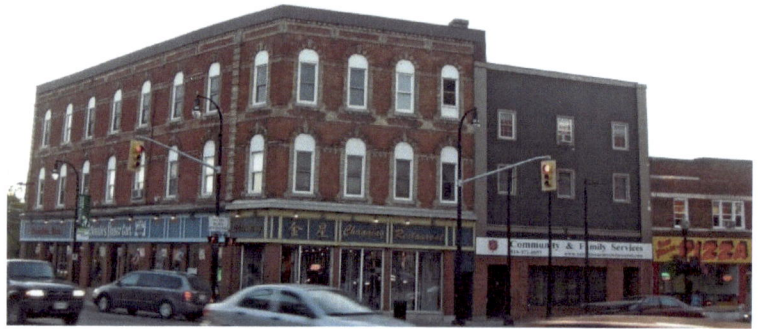

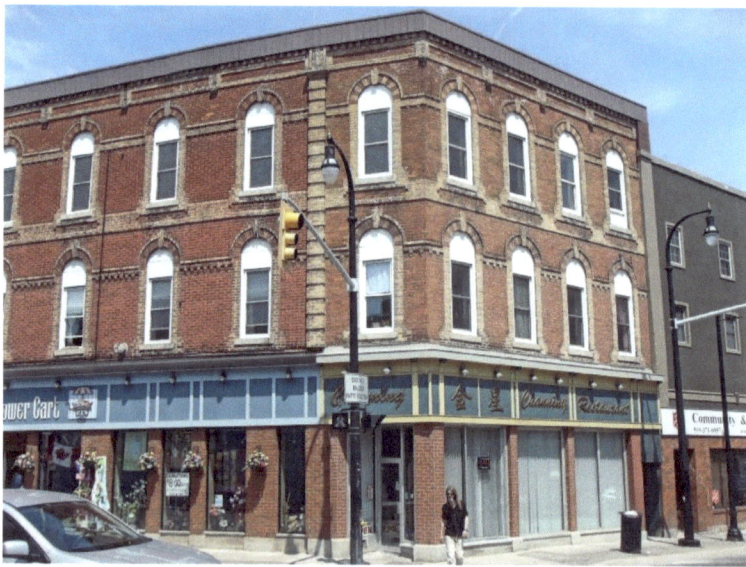

Dichromatic brickwork, keystones, dentil moulding, pilaster

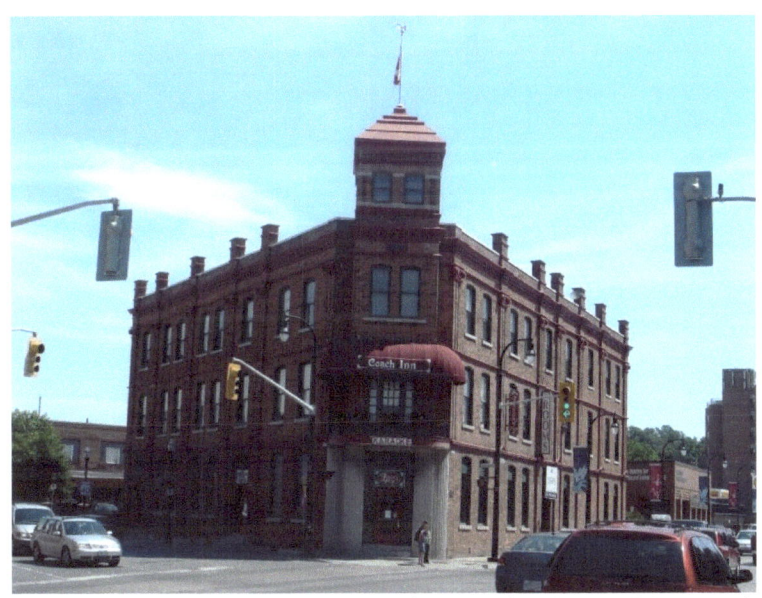

1005 Second Avenue East – Coach Inn - built in 1827 as a hotel
with 44 rooms, three parlours, bar, and dining room;
pilasters, dentil moulding

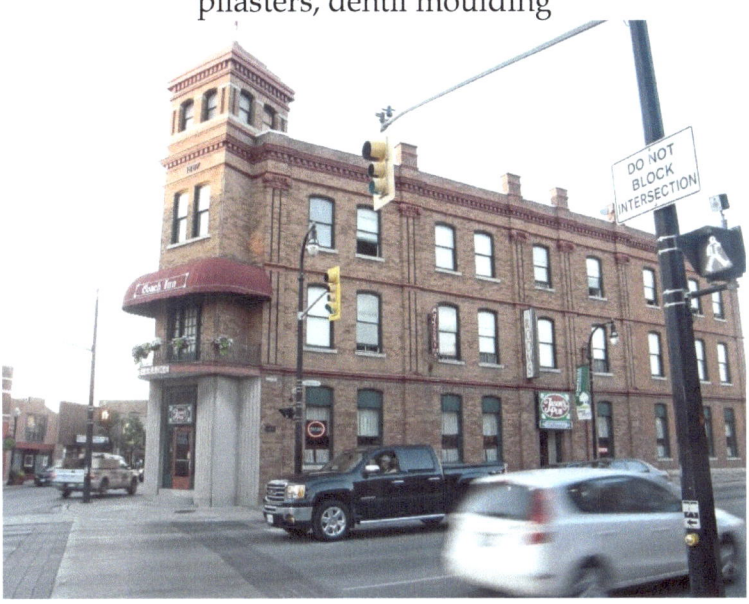

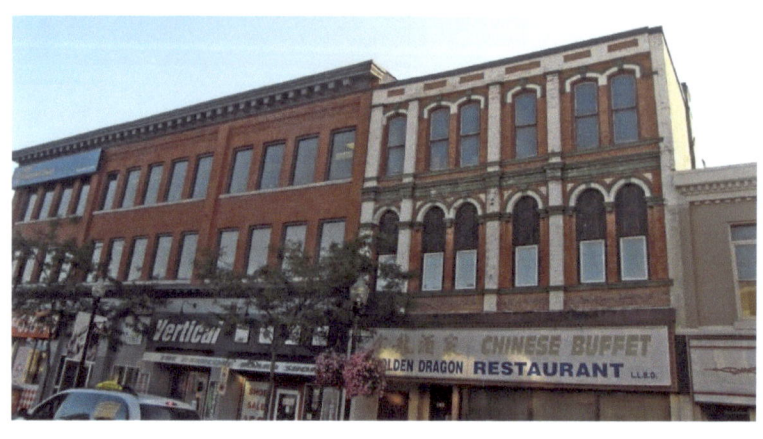

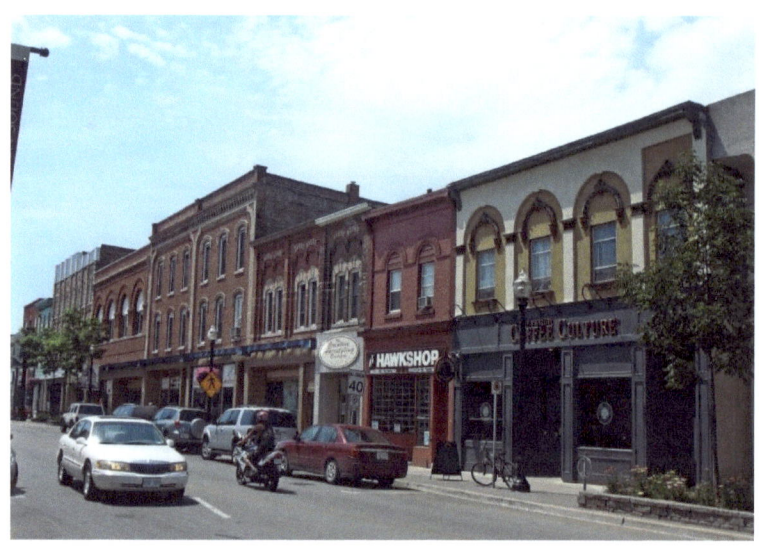

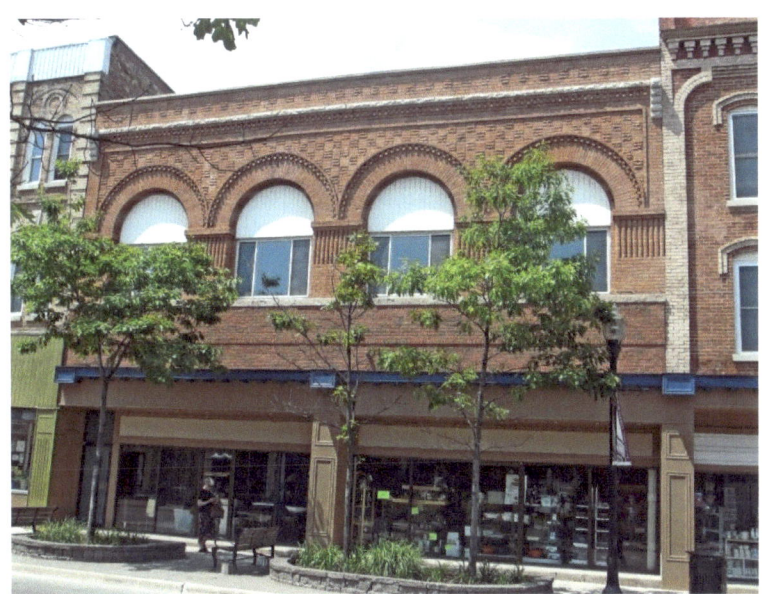

Romanesque style arches

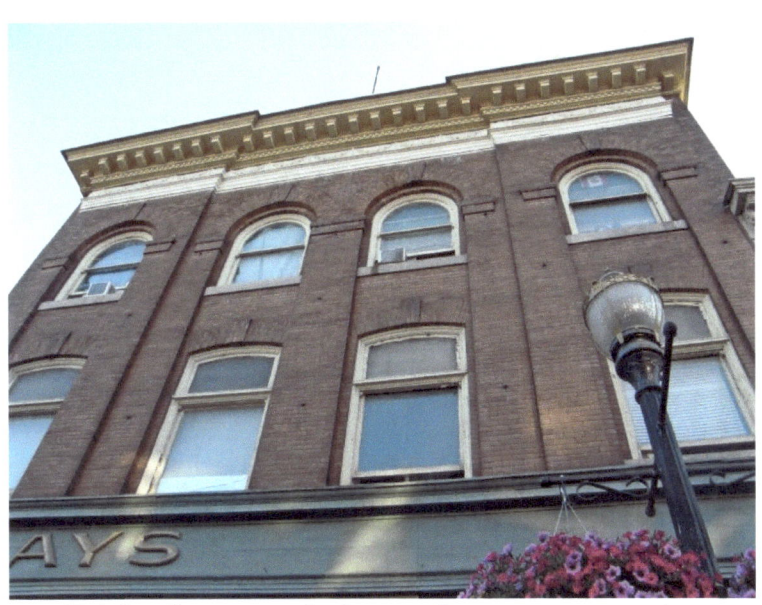

Brick pilasters, window arches, ornate cornice

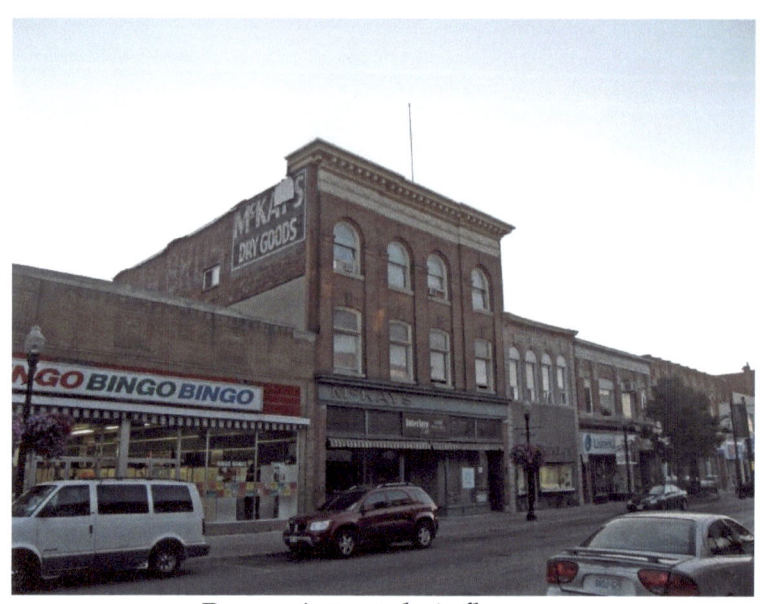

Beaux Arts style influence

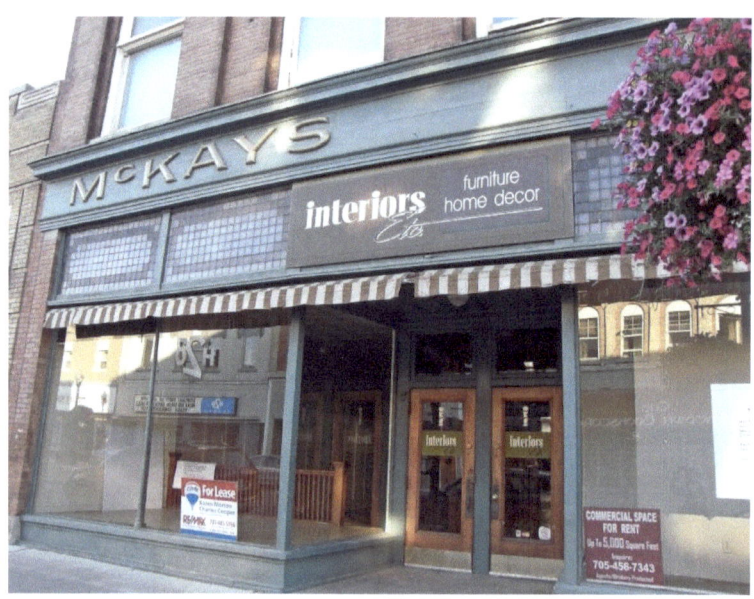

942 2nd Avenue East - G. B. Ryan & Co. 1905-1924
McKay Bros. Dry Goods 1924-1989

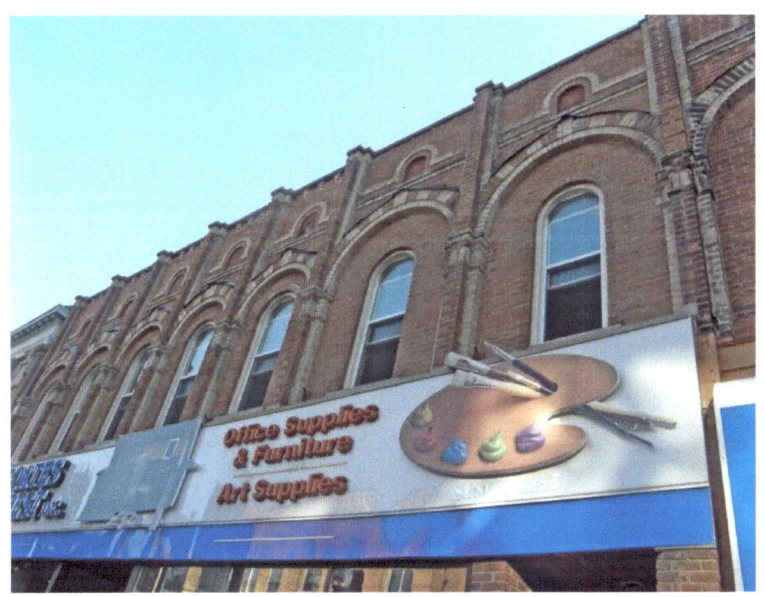

People's Department Store built in 1868 – pilasters, dichromatic brickwork

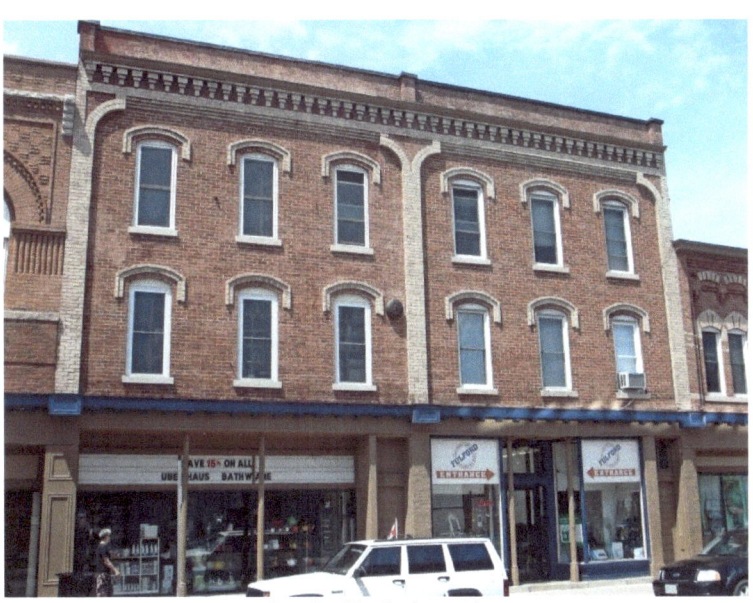

Corbelled dentils

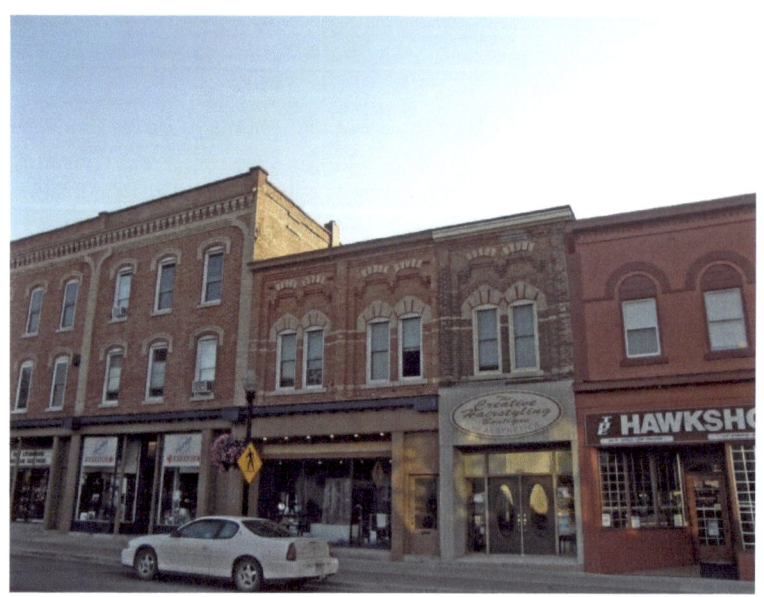

Brick pilasters, dichromatic brickwork

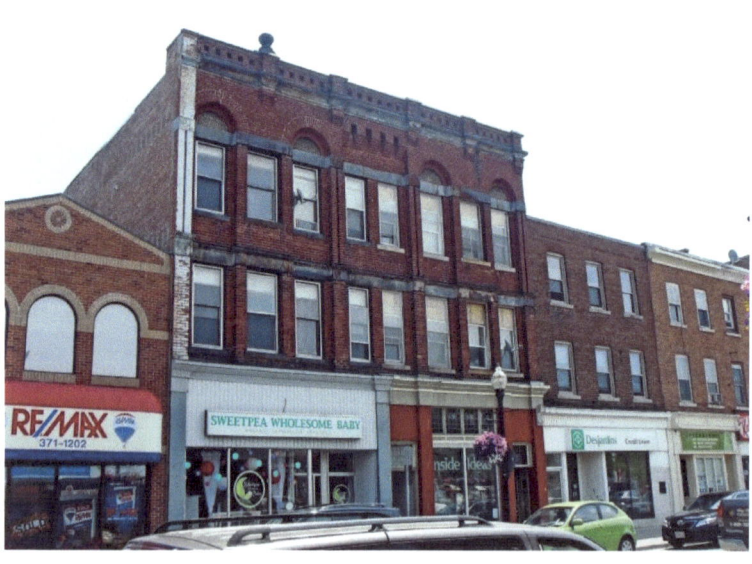

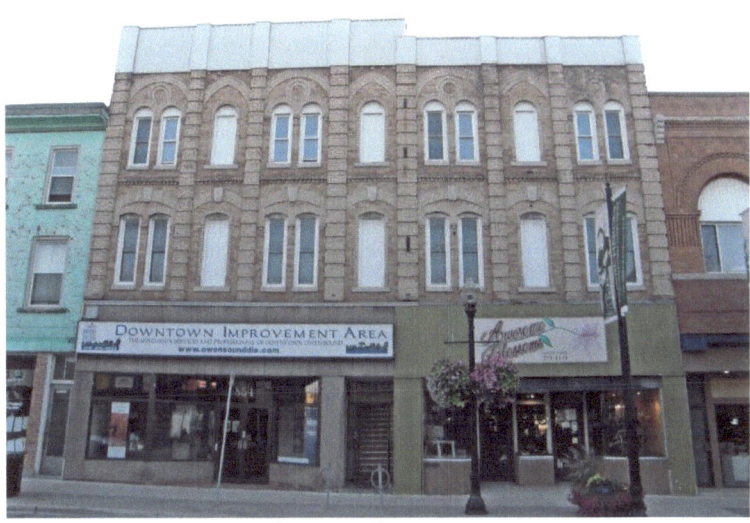

Pilasters, keystones

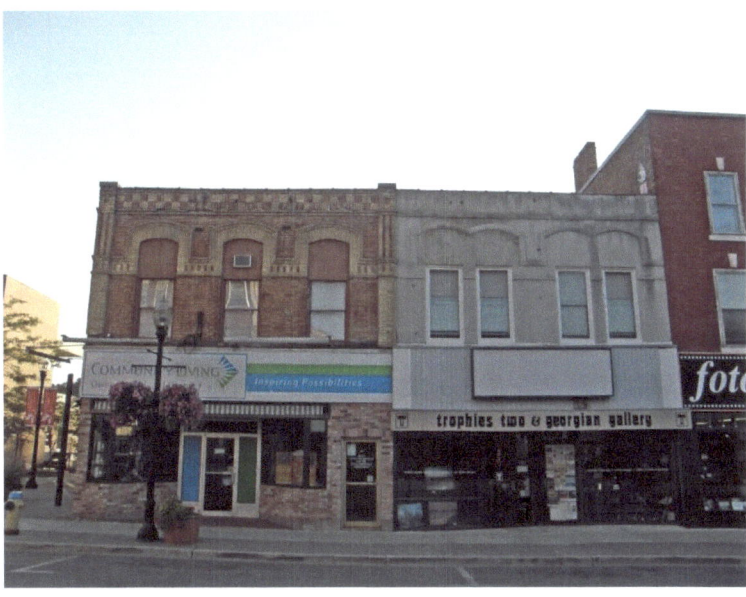

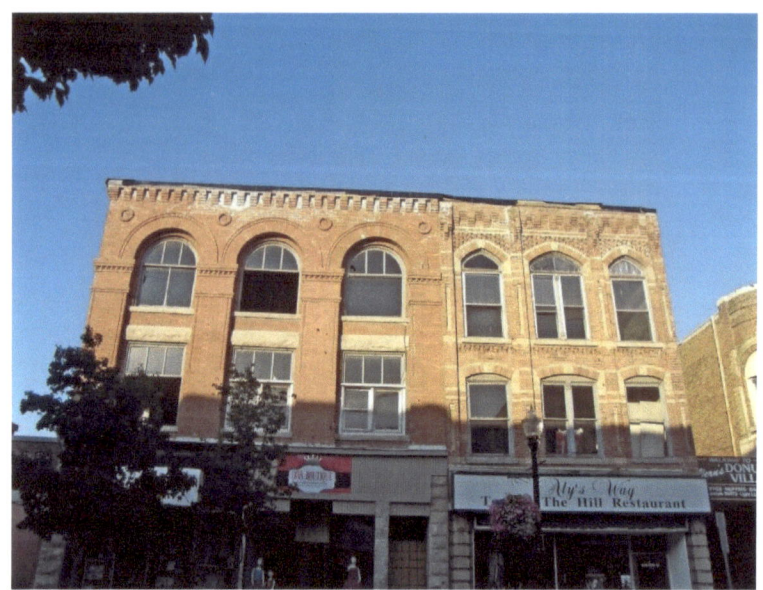

Corbelled dentils, pilasters with Romanesque style window arches on left of building

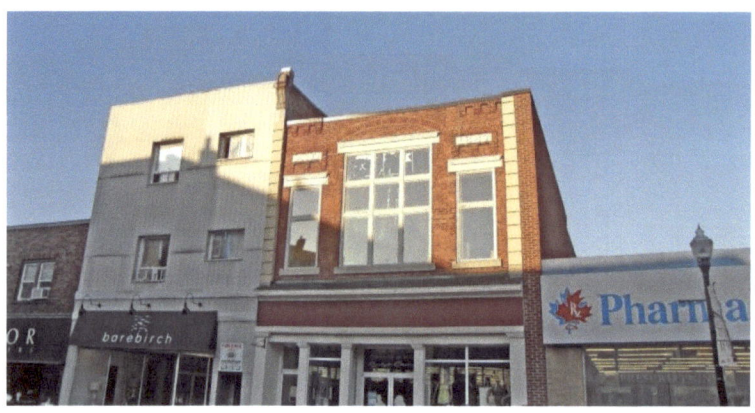

1887

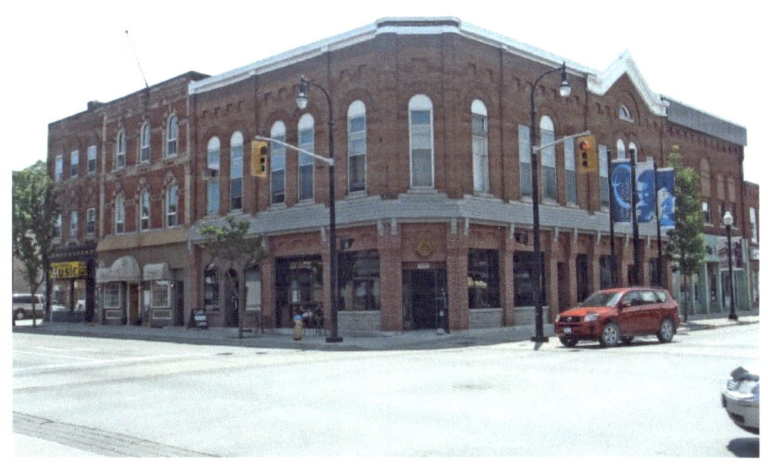

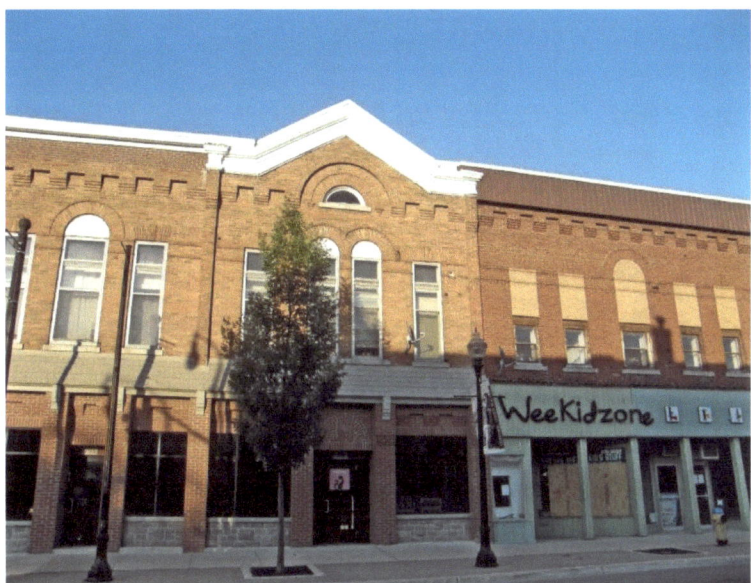

Corbelled dentils

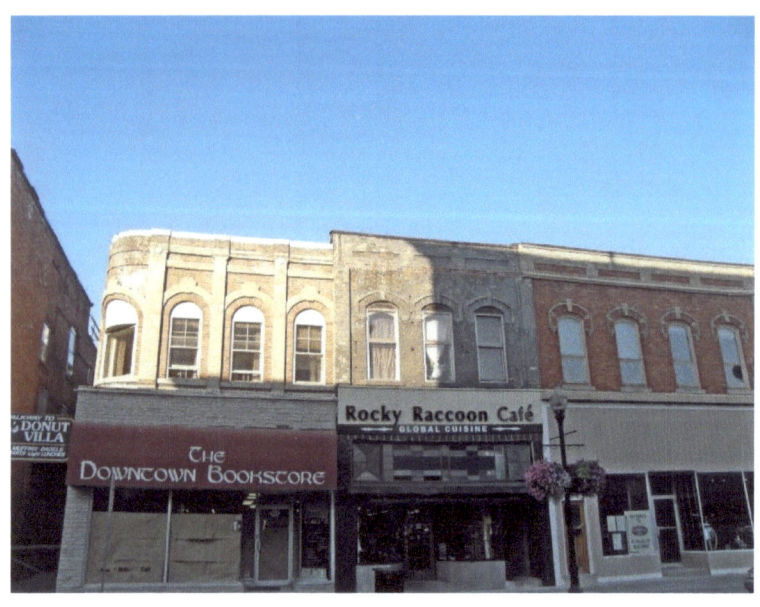

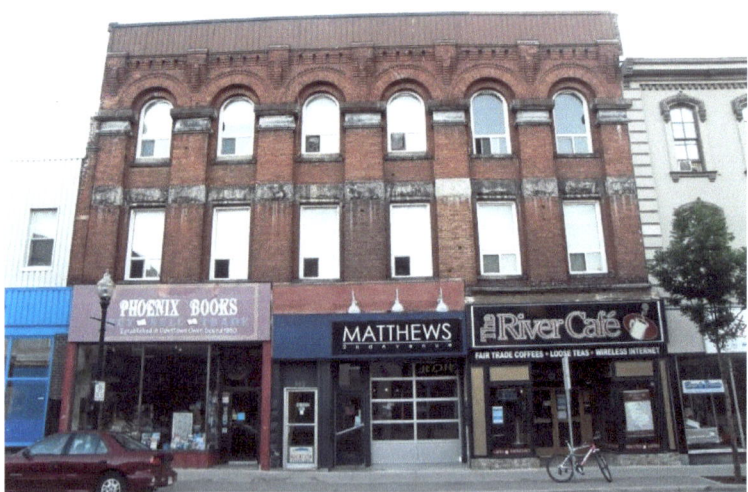

Pilasters, corbelled dentils, Romanesque style window arches

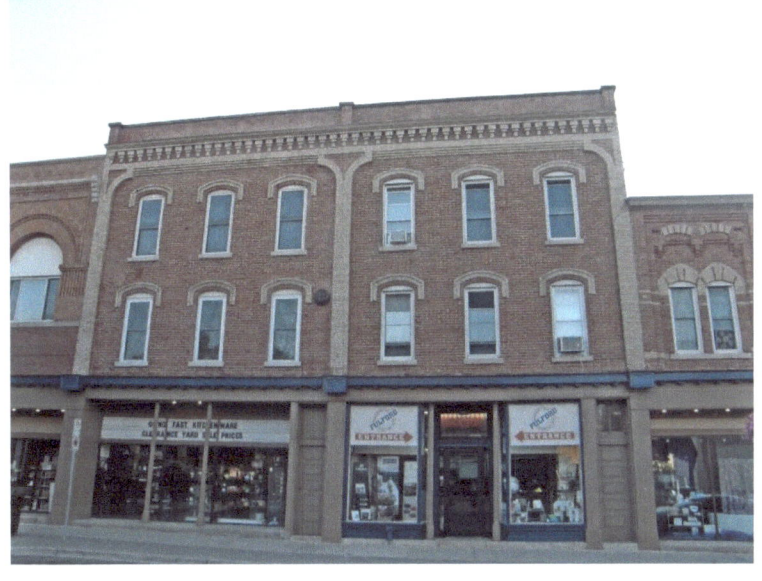

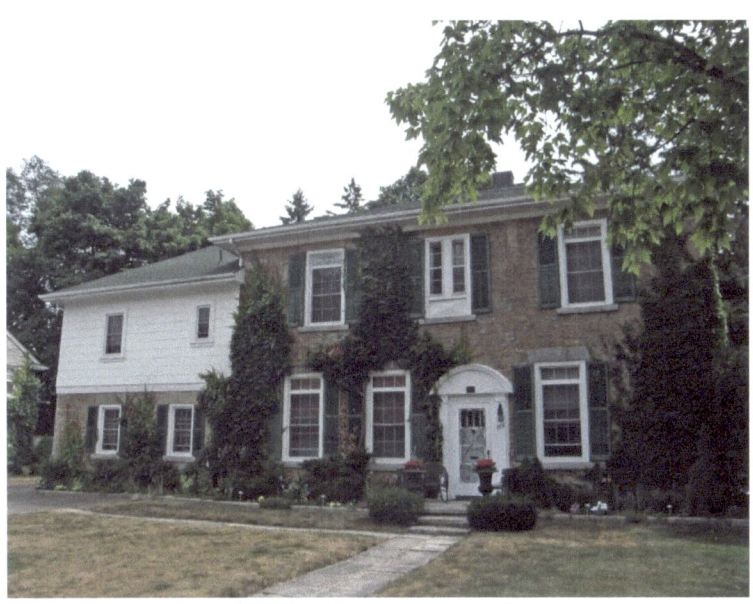

#805 – Georgian style

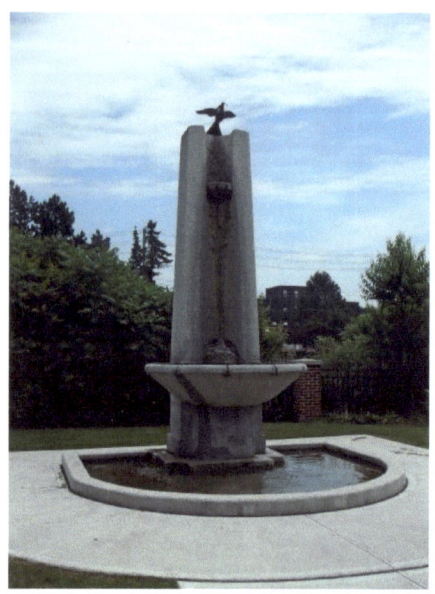
The Owen Sound Cenotaph

The Owen Sound Cenotaph was dedication on December 1, 1920 with 5,000 people lining both sides of the Sydenham River for its unveiling. The cenotaph is a unique example of Emmanuel Otto Hahn's work and it incorporates water trickling from the top down to a basin at the bottom where it streams through decorative channels to a pool at ground level. The monument is topped with a bronze dove holding an olive branch; a frog rests above the centre basin.

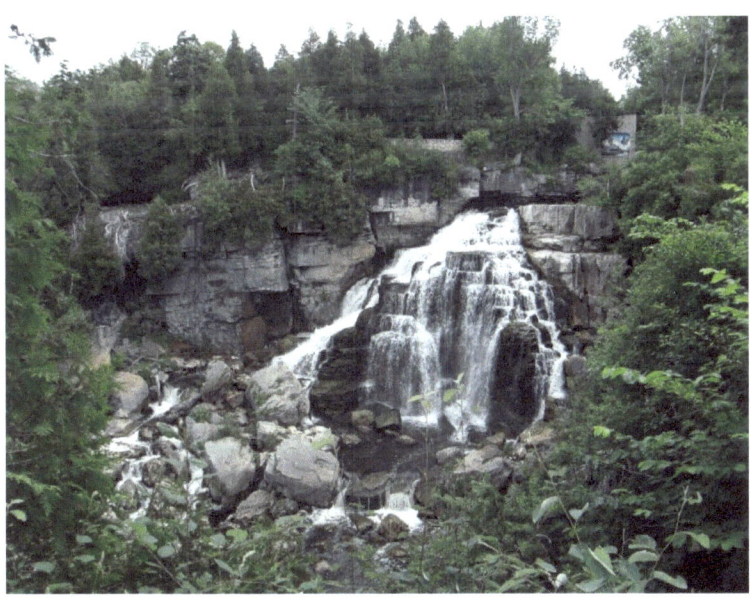

Inglis Falls – The Sydenham River pours over a fan-like rock formation of limestone shelves creating an eighteen metre high cascade that has carved a deep gorge at the base of the falls.

In 1845 Peter Inglis, a newly immigrated young Scottish millwright, bought the 300-acre property and built his gristmill on the very brink of the falls. It was powered by river water which was controlled and harnessed by a wooden dam, flume and water wheel. Inglis also used the river to power a sawmill which he built on the east side of the river opposite the gristmill.

Peter, his wife Ann with their three small children Eileen, John and George lived in a one storey frame house to the east of the mill until a larger two-storey stone house was built in 1852; three more children had been added to the family by this time, William, Mary Anne and Sarah. The small frame house, along with two others nearby, was used to house mill workers. At this time Inglis also built a new four-storey mill.

In the 1870s the sawmill at the falls was torn down and replaced by a woolen mill which produced cloth, flannels, and blankets.

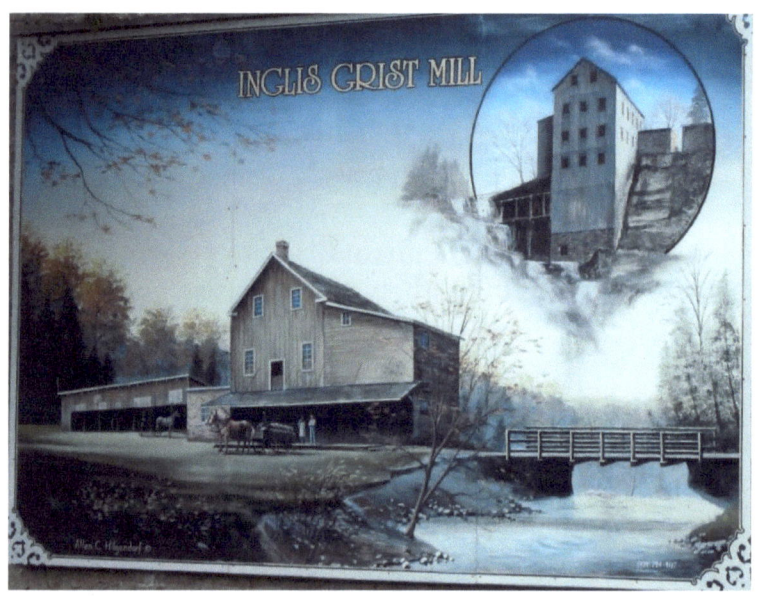

Black History

An estimated one-fourth of the blacks captured in Africa, destined for a life of slavery, crammed under horrible conditions in the holds of ships, died during the trip and never reached the New World.

By 1755 the thirteen colonies all legally recognized slavery as an institution. Many plantation owners placed specific orders for skilled slaves who already knew how to harvest rice, sugar and indigo. Most of the slaves who were transported were intelligent, skilled, cultured and already had their own firm set of spiritual beliefs. They were also skilled in the areas of blacksmithing, textiles, art and crafts. Many of these "secondary" skills remained hidden from the plantation owners.

In Canada slavery remained virtually nonexistent due to a short growing season and the economic impracticality of housing and feeding idle slaves over the winter months. Most of the slaves were servants for wealthy officials. Canadian households tended to have one slave or a very small number. Slaves usually served the same family during their lifetime. The British Imperial Act abolished slavery in the British Empire (including the Canadian colonies) and came into effective on August 1, 1834.

From about 1830 to the end of the American Civil War, escaped slaves made their way across the Canada-United States border via the Underground Railroad.
In 1850, a Fugitive Act passed in the United States made life more difficult for those of African descent, even the free Blacks in the Northern States. They could be kidnapped and sold as slaves in the South. Professional slave catchers could legally detain and hold anyone of African descent as a runaway slave; dogs were often used in the hunt for slaves. The Underground Railroad became busier as more slaves sought their freedom.

Slaves were not passive victims waiting to be rescued by white abolitionists. Slaves resisted the yoke of slavery and fought aggressively for their freedom and the right to maintain their African heritage. The struggle to be free was constant. Becoming free meant more than a change of residence to a slave; once on the road to choosing their own destiny, slaves had to make the emotional transition from being an enslaved person to becoming a free one.

The earliest escape attempts were made by individual slaves and these escapes formed the paths and trails that led to the Underground Railroad. Stories of the almost non-existent slavery north of the border were taken back home by United States Army soldiers after the War of 1812. These stories encouraged slaves to make a break for freedom. Because of the secrecy of the Underground Railroad, written records of those who took this route to freedom do not exist. It is estimated that between 40,000 and 100,000 slaves escaped on the Underground Railroad.

Safe houses offered shelter and nourishment along the route, but were changed often to avoid detection. "Agents", "conductors", and "station masters" provided shelter, food, money, directions, means of transportation, and changes of clothes. Often slaves escaped in disguise — men wore women's clothes, and women wore men's clothes. Light-skinned Blacks dressed as upper class white citizens travelling with their entourage of "slaves". Crates labelled "dry goods" concealed runaway slaves. They were hidden in secret spaces in homes, in secret compartments in wagons and in the hulls of boats. They hid by day, travelling under the darkness of night. They swam rivers, crossed frozen rivers on foot and on horseback, and walked long distances. They slept in barns, in fields, and in woods. Most of the Underground Railroad routes travelled north, following the North Star, eventually ending in Canada.

Secrecy on the slaves' part was the main ingredient that made the Underground Railroad work. Warning signals and escape messages were used in conjunction with the Railroad in the form of spirituals, phrases and quilt patterns. Even the continuing threat of recriminations could not stop the slaves from singing spirituals. The Underground Railroad was sometimes referred to as the "Gospel Train". In the slaves' world of intolerance and suspicion on the part of their white owners, secrecy and coded communication was a necessity of everyday life. It is the aftermath of slavery and the deep lack of trust created that have prevented the code of silence from being broken and the stories told. Even the youngest child was taught not to repeat secrets outside of the family circle. Many headed for the Village of Sydenham (Owen Sound), the last terminal of the Railroad and settled here, finding work and raising families. Many of Owen Sound's Black citizens were trailblazers, famous beyond the City's borders. Others are local heroes whose stories have educated and inspired several generations of Owen Sounders. Their courage and hard work contributed to the growth of Grey County and the City of Owen Sound.

The Underground Railroad cannot be viewed as solely a Black story. It is a universal story, based on the human need for individual freedom and is not restricted to any one skin colour. Blacks and whites worked together in an organization based on implicit trust and secrecy; the betrayal by whites or even another slave was a constant threat to escaping slaves and their supporters. It is an integral part of Owen Sound's history, and of Canadian history as well, for the role it played in the development of both the City and the country and their citizens.

In honour of these settlers, a commemorative Cairn in Harrison Park was unveiled on July 31, 2004 at the annual Emancipation Picnic. The picnic has been held every year since 1862, and celebrates the British Commonwealth Emancipation Act of August 1, 1834 and the United States Emancipation Proclamation of January 1, 1863.

Through symbolism and interpretive plaques, the Cairn traces the route of those abducted from their native Africa, forced into slavery in the West Indies and the United States, and how many escaped to Canada via a network called the Underground Railroad.

Black History Cairn

Quilt Squares – Hidden signs and coded messages told slaves of the methods and means to find freedom. Concealed in the quilt patterns, complex and detailed instructions were passed to the escaping slaves. These quilts hung over railings or clotheslines. The patterns could be mixed in a sampler quilt, containing numerous messages, or held a repeated pattern to share clear directions. Some of the most common patterns include:

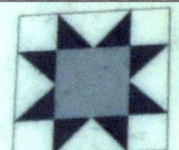	North Star: Use the North Star as a compass point and follow it north to Canada and freedom.
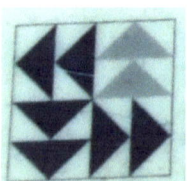	Flying Geese: The darkest triangle symbolized both geese and the escaping slaves. The viewer used these arrows to learn which direction to go next. Often the geese pointed directly north to freedom. The slaves knew the geese flew north in the spring and south in the fall.

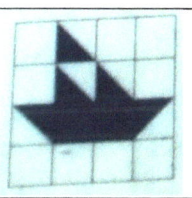	Sailboat: This message indicated that a large body of water lay ahead and needed to be crossed.
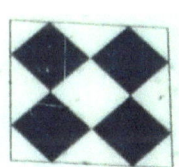	Crossroads: This pattern had many interpretations. It could indicate that the path crossed with another, and warned of the potential danger of people who may be travelling the other road. It was also used to represent Cleveland, Ohio.
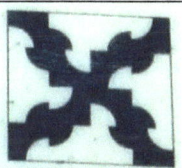	Drunkard's Path: The route ahead held many obstacles, requiring the traveller to backtrack, stay off main roads, cross streams or rivers, and to follow a circuitous route.
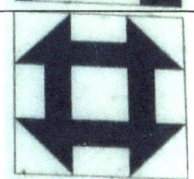	Monkey Wrench: This message advised the viewer to gather up tools and family and prepare for the escape to freedom. The image is an African symbol using only the sun and the stars as reference points.
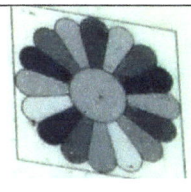	Dresden Plate: This image referred to both Dresden, Ontario as a rest stop and Dresden, Ontario as a safe place to settle. In some cases it also indicated the need to travel by cart.
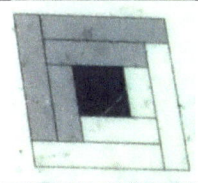	Log Cabin: The dark or yellow central square indicated a safe house where the fugitive could rest.

The cairn abounds in symbolism. Each piece reflects a particular aspect of the Underground Railroad and the stories of those associated with it. The cairn as a whole calls for quiet meditation and reflection on the experiences of these brave pioneers.

	Church: Faith sustained people in times of need and crisis, through the trials of slavery and the hardships of settlement. Copied from the original windows of the first black church in Owen Sound, the windows in the cairn bare testament to the strength and vision of early black settlers here.
	Ruins: The ruined wall of the cairn reflects the changing status of the first black pioneers. As they tore down the oppressive walls of slavery, they began construction of a new life and new home for themselves in Canada.
	Apple Trees: Some people used the blossoming apple trees as signposts in their quest to escape slavery. The blossoming season occurs later as one heads north, finally arriving in Canada. Many of these settlers took up farming in their new home and the apple trees testify to those early patterns of settlements.
	The River: Beyond the cairn lies the north-flowing Sydenham River. The river flows in the direction of freedom, the emancipation that these brave pioneers sought in their struggle to liberate themselves from oppression and servitude.

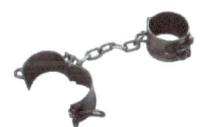 Broken Shackles: Symbolic of the chain of oppression and tyranny the black settlers faced in slavery, these broken shackles in the cairn lay bare the terror of the past, and the joy of freedom.

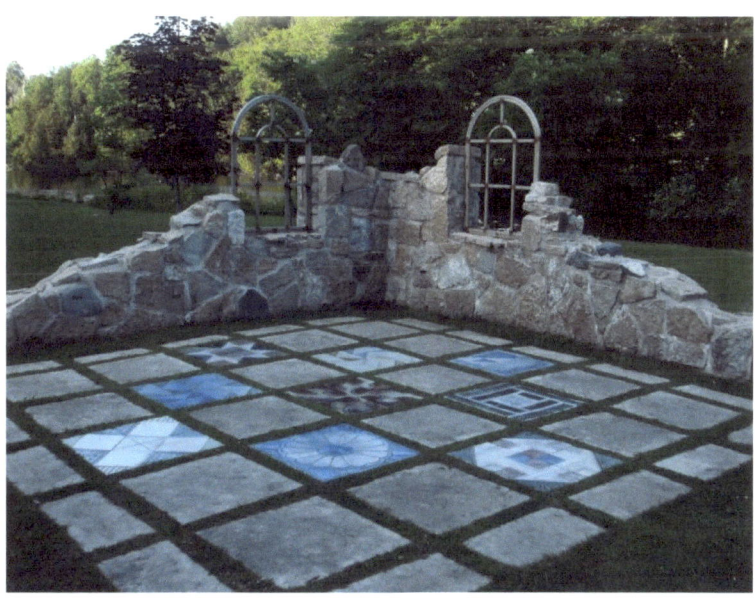

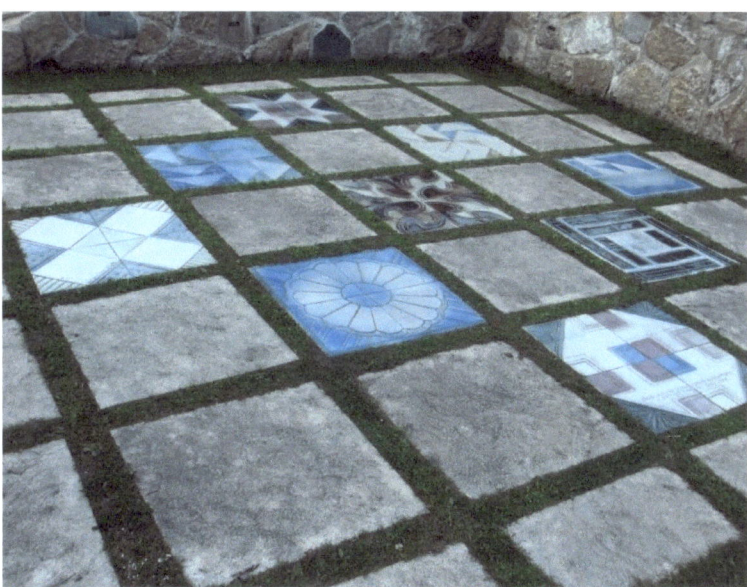

Harrison Park

John Harrison, born in Staffordshire England, emigrated to Canada at the age of six with his widowed father, three sisters and three brothers. It was 1830 and they settled in Puslinch Township near Guelph. Eighteen years later, John and two brothers, William and Robert, arrived in the Village of Sydenham (now Owen Sound). They acquired the mill dam site on the Sydenham River and operated waterpower grist, woollen and saw mills. In 1866, John moved his sawmill to the Pottawatomi River and established the steam powered Owen Sound Saw Mills. He prospered and expanded the saw and planning mills and the range of products offered. In 1861 he married Emma Hart and they raised their family of six children in a white roughcast house beside his mills. In 1875-76 they purchased the land now known as Harrison Park. The mill operation included horses. When the mills were slack in depressed times, John sent the men to work and exercise the teams on this land. They built roads, bridges, paths and buildings, gradually bringing his vision for the parkland to life. John and his family and employees transformed this land and created Harrison Pleasure Grounds where everyone was welcome. Between 1909-1911 while John's eldest son Frederick served as Mayor of Owen Sound, the parkland was transferred to the town for half the value of the land – as long as it remained a public park forever.

The park today includes picnic facilities, basketball courts, heated twin swimming pools, canoe and paddle boat rentals for use on the river, a bird sanctuary, a mini-putt golf course, playground, campsites, cycling and walking trails, and the black history cairn and Freedom Trail.

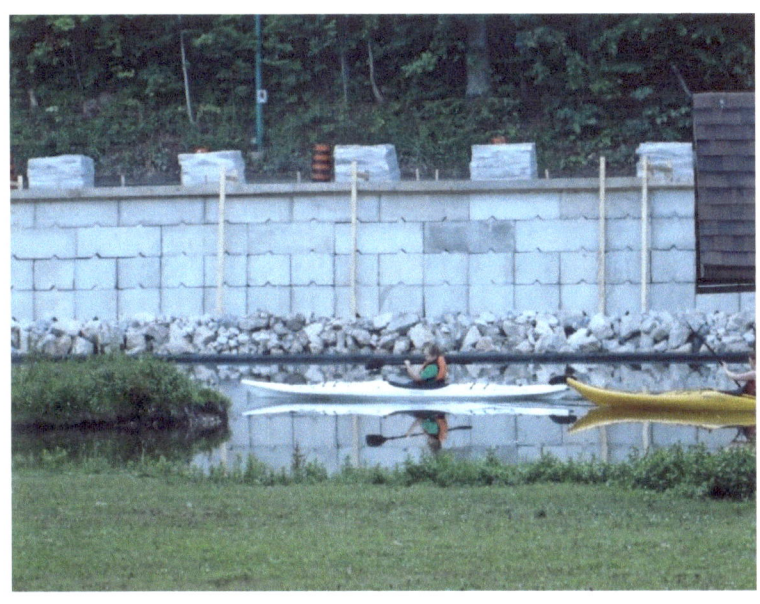

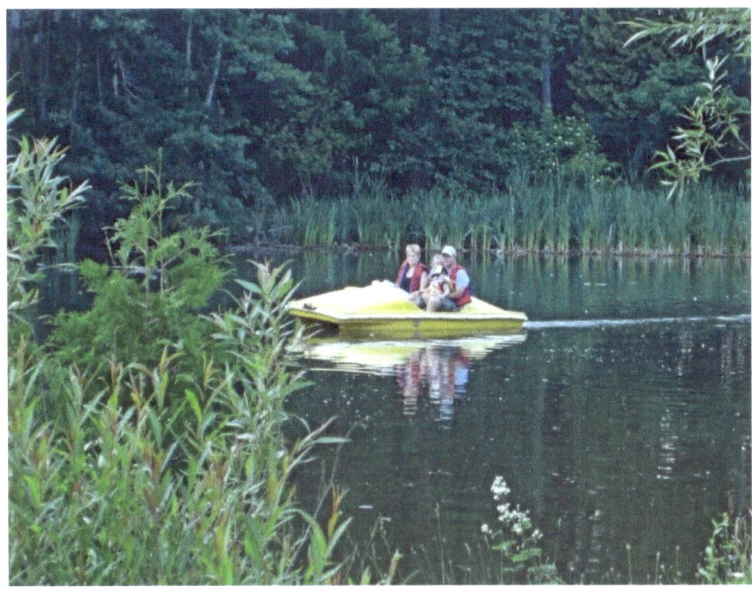

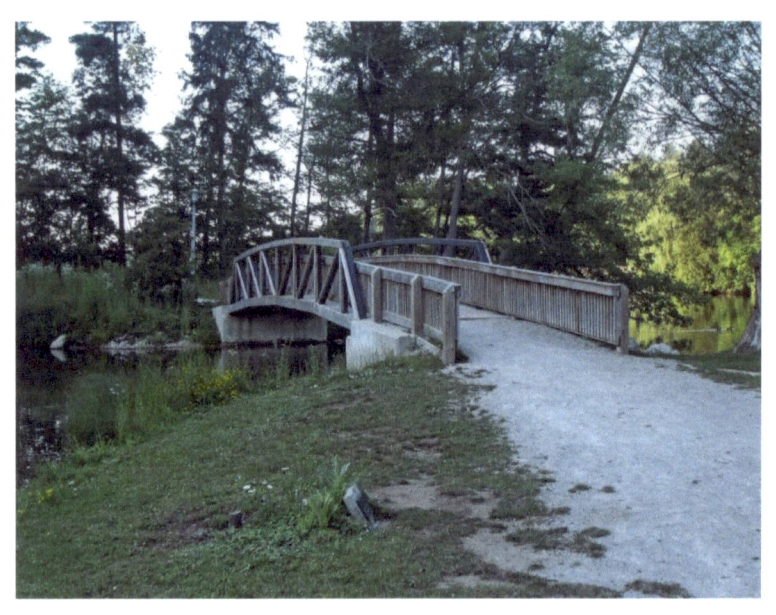

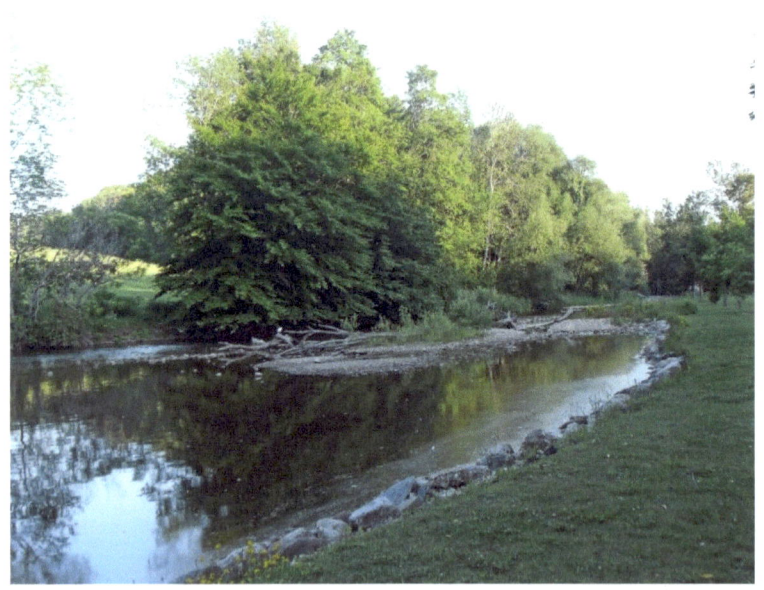

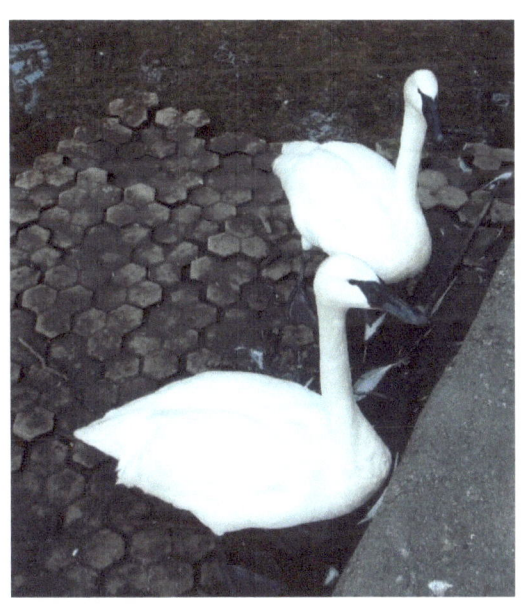

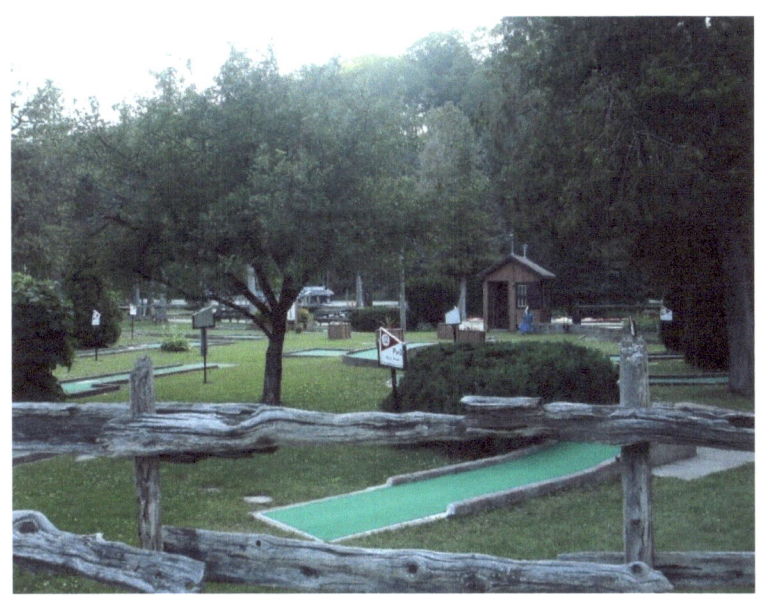

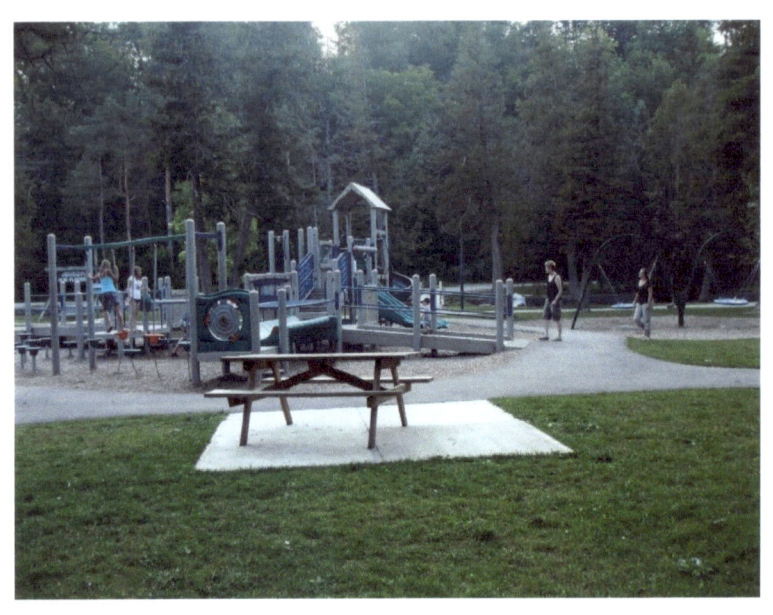

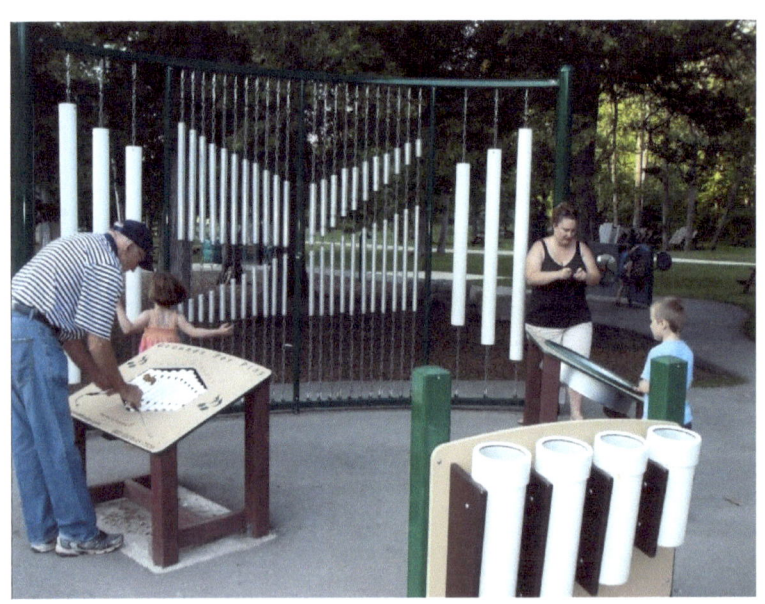

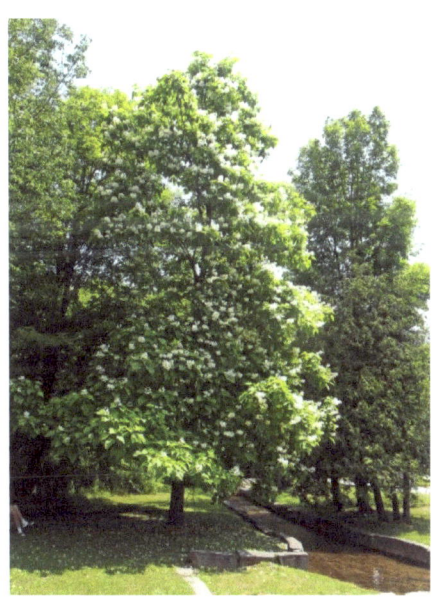

Chestnut tree in bloom

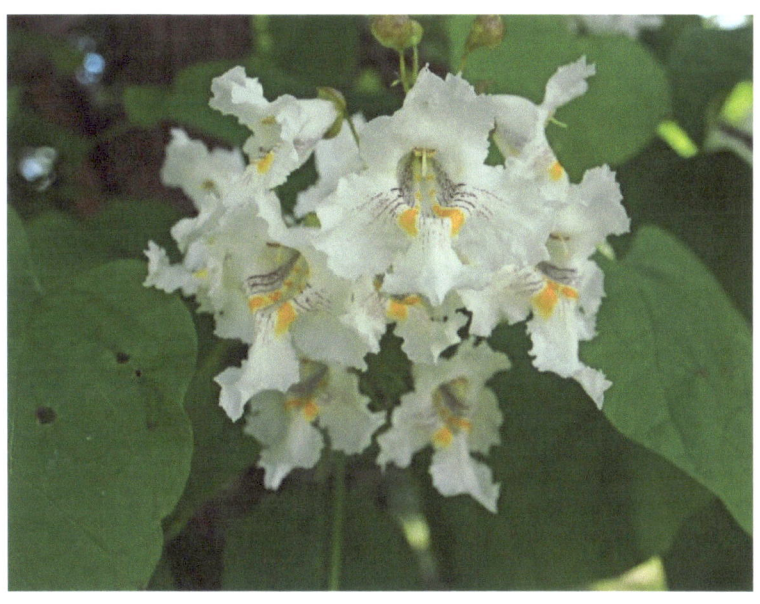

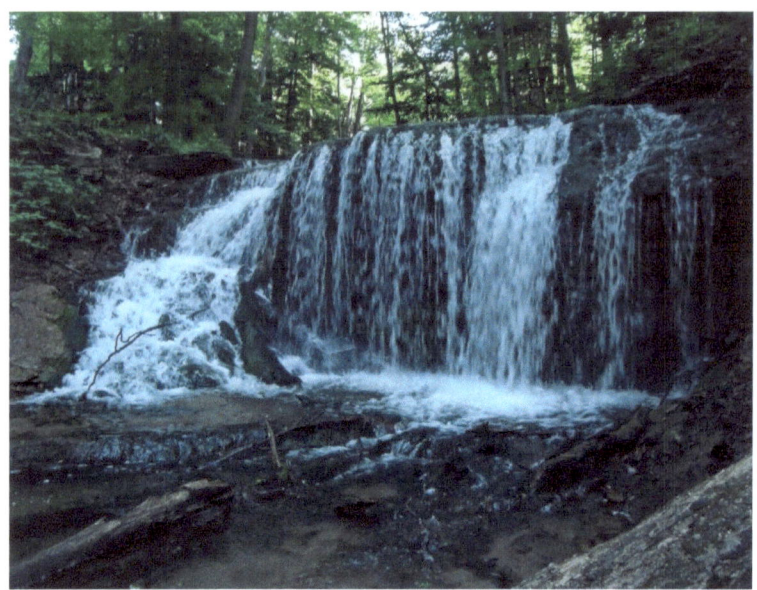

The falls on Weavers Creek in Harrison Park is an opportunity to see a miniature plunge falls flanked by cascading falls – two types of waterfalls in one.

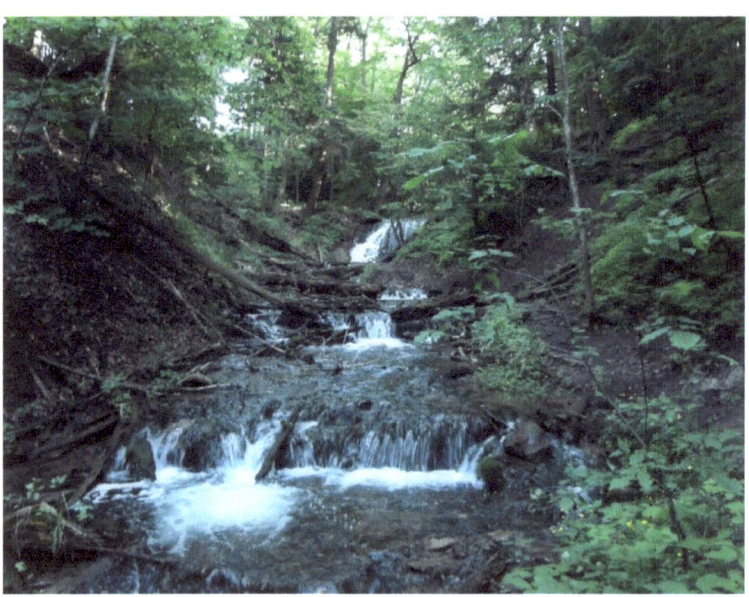

Weaver's Creek feeds into Sydenham River.

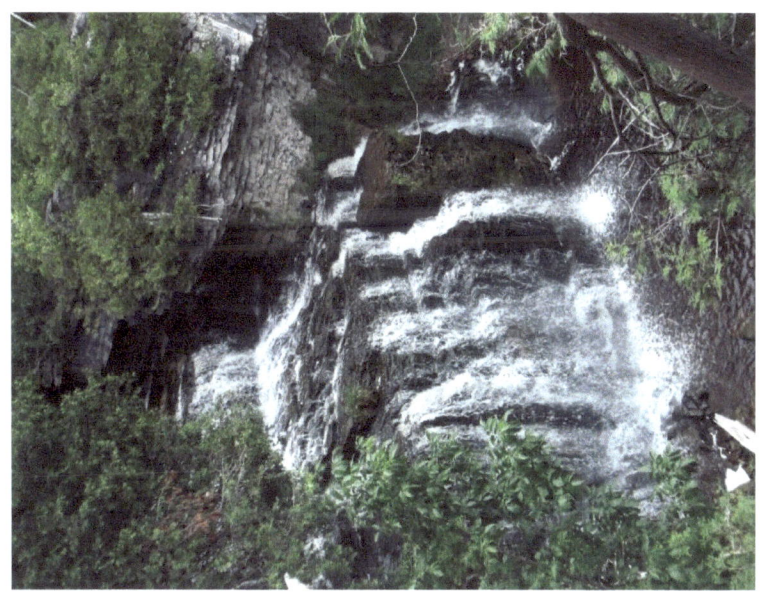

Jones Falls, Springmount – the Pottawatomi River cascades 12 metres over the Niagara Escarpment

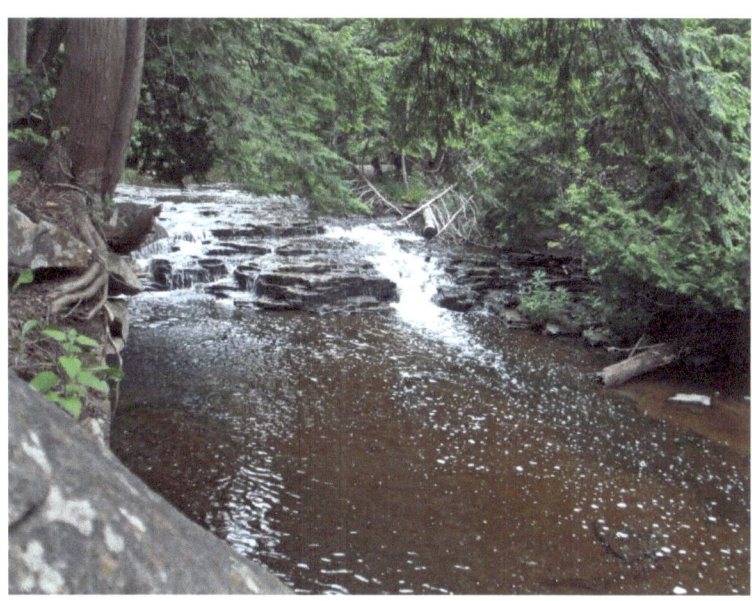

Architectural Terms

Banding: Different materials, colours or textures used in horizontal bands along a wall. Example: see Page 22	
Brackets: a decorative or weight-bearing structural element which forms a right angle with one side against a wall and the other under a projecting surface such as an eave or roof. Example: see Page 23	
Buttress: a masonry structure built against or projecting from a wall which serves to support or reinforce the wall. In Canadian architecture, they are sometimes used for decoration. Example: Knox United Church (see Page 16)	
Cornice: originally the wooden overhang of the roof. With the use of stone, brick, iron and steel, the cornice is any projecting shelf at the top of a ceiling or roof. They can be very decorative. Example: 942 2nd Avenue East (see Page 31)	
Cornice Return: decorative element on the end of a gable. Example: see Page 24	
Cupola: A domed or curved roof rising from a building as a decorative element. Example:	
Dentil Moulding: an even series of rectangles used as ornamental decoration in cornices. Example: see Page 33 – corbelled dentils	

Dichromatic brickwork: the use of two colours of brick, tile or slate to decorate a façade. Example: see Page 34	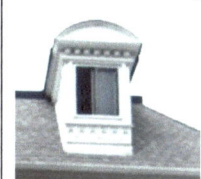
Dormer: (French for "sleep") a gable end window that pierces through the plane of a sloping roof surface to create usable space in the top floor or attic of a building by adding headroom. Example: see Page 22	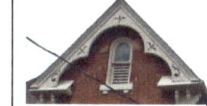
Gable: the triangular portion of a wall between the edges of a sloping roof. Example: see Page 25	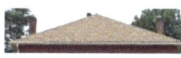
Hipped Roof: a roof where all sides slope downwards to the walls with no gables. Example: see Page 10	
Keystones and Voussoirs: a voussoir is a wedge-shaped element used in building an arch. A keystone is the central stone that locks all the stones into position, allowing the arch to bear weight. A keystone is often enlarged and embellished. Example: see Page 28	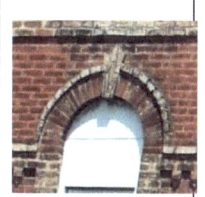
Lancet Window: a tall, narrow window with a pointed arch at its top. Example: see Page 16	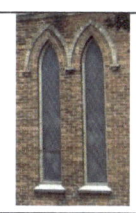

Mansard Roof: This style was popularized by Francois Mansart (1598-1666), an accomplished architect of the French Baroque period and especially fashionable during the Second French Empire (1852-1870). This roof is almost flat on the top section, with two slopes on each of its sides with the lower slope at a steeper angle than the upper and having dormer windows. Example: Old Post Office (see Page 26)	
Palladian Window: a large window that is divided into three sections with the centre section larger than the two side sections and usually arched. Example: see Page 23	
Pediment: a triangular section above the horizontal structure (entablature), typically supported by columns. The inside of the triangle is called the tympanum. Example: Old Post Office (see Page 26)	
Pilaster: a slightly projecting column built into or applied to the face of a wall for additional structural support. Example: Coach Inn – see Page 29	
Quoin: masonry blocks at the corner of a wall, often a decorative feature, usually larger or of a different colour than the rest of the wall. Example: see Page 25	

Rose Window: a circular window with ornamental tracery radiating from the centre. Example: Knox United Church	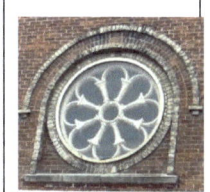
Turret: a small tower that projects from the wall of a building. Example: 935 2nd Avenue West (see Page 12)	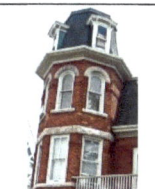
Vergeboard and Finial: also called bargeboards – hang from the projecting end of a roof and are often elaborately carved and ornamented. **Finial:** ornament added to the top of a gable, pinnacle, canopy or spire – a Gothic element. Example: see Page 20	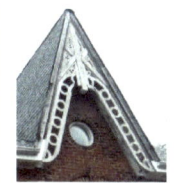

Beaux Arts: Promoters of this style sought to express the classical principles on a grand and imposing scale. Many of the Beaux Arts buildings were banks, post offices, and railway stations. The Ontario Beaux Arts style is eclectic mixing elements of Classical, Renaissance and Baroque. Often the designs have a temple-like façade, pedimented porticos, balustrades, capitals in many styles. Example: Old Post Office	
Edwardian, 1900-1930 – This style bridges the ornate and elaborate styles of the Victorian era and the simplified styles of the 20th century. Balanced facades, simple roof lines, dormer windows, large front porches, and smooth brick surfaces are its characteristics. Example: see Page 23	
Georgian, before 1860 – This style began with the British King Georges in the 18th century. These buildings have balanced facades around a central door, medium-pitched gable roofs, and small paned windows. Example: see Page 39	
Gothic Revival, 1830-1890 – These decorative buildings have sharply-pitched gables with highly detailed verge boards, pointed-arch window openings, and dichromatic brickwork. It is a common style in Ontario. Example: see Page 13	

Italianate, 1850-1900 – It has wide-bracketed eaves, belvederes, wrap-around verandahs. Example: see Page 10	
Queen Anne, 1885-1900 – This style is distinguished by an irregular outline featuring a combination of an offset tower, broad gables, projecting two-storey bays, verandahs, multi-sloped roofs, and tall, decorative chimneys. A mixture of brick and wood is common. Windows often have one large single-paned bottom sash and small panes in the upper sash. Example: see Page 18	
Romanesque Revival, 1880-1910 – This style hearkens back to medieval architecture of the 11th and 12th centuries with a heavy appearance, blocky towers and rounded arches. Example: see Page 38 (arch)	
Second Empire, 1860-1880 – The mansard roof is the most noteworthy feature of this style and is evidence of the French origins. Projecting central towers and one or two-storey bays can also be present. Example: 935 2nd Avenue West (see Page 12)	
Tudor Revival – exposed timbers with stucco infill, multi-paned windows. Example: see Page 11	

Vernacular architecture is based on local needs, construction materials and reflecting local traditions...a building designed by an amateur without any training in design; the individual will have been guided by a series of conventions built up in his locality, paying little attention to what may be fashionable. The function of the building would be the dominant factor, aesthetic considerations, though present to some small degree, being quite minimal. Local materials would be used as a matter of course, other materials being chosen and imported quite exceptionally. Example: see Page 11

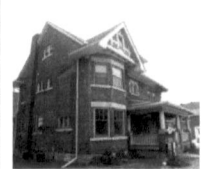

www.ingramcontent.com/pod-product-compliance
Lightning Source LLC
Chambersburg PA
CBHW040844180526
45159CB00001B/316